DANCING TO ZION

Smyth & Helwys Publishing
6316 Peake Road
Macon, Georgia 31210-3960
1-800-747-3016

Library of Congress Cataloging-in-Publication Data

Names: Edwards, Judson, author.
Title: Dancing to Zion : how to harvest joy on the road to heaven / by Judson
Edwards.
Description: Macon : Smyth & Helwys, 2016. | Originally published: Grand
Rapids, Mich. : Zondervan Pub. House, c1986.
Identifiers: LCCN 2016037996 | ISBN 9781573129022
Subjects: LCSH: Christian life--Baptist authors.
Classification: LCC BV4501.3 .E3957 2016 | DDC 248.4/861--dc23
LC record available at https://lccn.loc.gov/2016037996

JUDSON EDWARDS

DANCING
to
ZION

How to Harvest Joy on the
Road to Heaven

Also by *Judson Edwards*

A Matter of Choice
Running the Race
Dancing to Zion
The Coffee Pot Letters
The Case of the Uptight Christian
Relationship Therapy
The Leadership Labyrinth
Hidden Treasures
Making the Good News Good Again
Blissful Affliction
Quiet Faith
Bugles in the Afternoon

To Sherry,
my partner in the dance of life

Contents

Introduction

We're marching to Zion,
Beautiful, beautiful Zion;
We're marching upward to Zion,
The beautiful city of God.

I have no serious quarrel with Isaac Watts, who penned the words to that hymn in 1707. I have every confidence that I really am marching, or at least shuffling, to Zion, so I can sing it with a certain amount of conviction. I can also sing with moderate fervor the other "warfare" songs of the faith: "Am I a Soldier of the Cross," "The Banner of the Cross," "Fight the Good Fight," and "Onward Christian Soldiers."

But I do confess that the marching, militant message of those hymns no longer stirs my deepest feelings. Frankly, I'm now tired of marching. For years I've been marching to Sunday school classes, worship services, prayer meetings, evangelism seminars, and other "spiritual" activities. The thought of any more marching—even to Zion, the heavenly city—is not too enticing.

I am now discovering, firsthand, that too much marching makes for weary pilgrims. When the Christian life is a military march, the soldiers eventually become somber and sapped. Church becomes more funeral than festival; prayer becomes obligation instead of celebration; the Bible becomes a strategy manual instead of a love letter. The recent surge of books dealing with Christian "burnout" is a telltale sign that marching is taking its toll on the troops. And I fear, after nearly thirty years as a Christian and twelve as a pastor, I too could find myself on the casualty list.

What I need now is not marching but dancing. I could sing the old hymn with even more enthusiasm if we could sing "We're Dancing to Zion." In fairness to Isaac Watts, his hymn is actually a song brimming with joy and celebration. Remember the first verse?

Come, we that love the Lord,
And let our joys be known;

Join in a song with sweet accord,
Join in a song with sweet accord,
And thus surround the throne,
And thus surround the throne.

The whole song is a hymn of praise that stands on tiptoe to behold the glory of heaven. But marching? No... dancing! That captures the mood of the hymn better for me.

This book is my attempt to see the Christian pilgrimage more as a dance than a march. I'm writing these ideas for myself and for people like me: faithful Christians who are weary from years of marching; inquisitive Christians who yearn for something fresh; stagnant Christians who long to go deeper into the things of the Spirit; burned-out Christians who wonder where God went.

I hope that somewhere in the pages that follow, my frustrations, experiences, discoveries, and dreams will intersect yours and that together we can then chuckle at the unbelievably Good News that is ours in Christ. I hope to write something here that will enable both of us to go dancing to Zion.

I.
DANCING TO A
DIFFERENT TUNE

I wonder if there are soft-spoken voices who deliver assignments to all of us at various times, and if my problem is one of hearing too acutely. It is nice to think that I have company—that others dance to the muted music I hear.
W. P. Kinsella in Shoeless Joe

1.
Memoirs of a Serious Christian

Memory is a funny thing. My grandfather, always known for his keen mind, now sits in a nursing home, bewildered by the tricks his memory plays on him. The last time I visited him, he could not remember the names of his four sons. He recalled in minute detail, however, the purchase of forty acres of farm land in 1922. It is as if Time has walked through the memory compartment of his brain, randomly erasing some tapes and turning up the volume on others.

I must have some of the affliction myself. When I look back and try to plot the vital points of my spiritual graph, I am astonished at the trivia that comes to mind. Why do I remember these things? Why has Time already erased so many sermons, moments of decision, and important people? And why has it turned up the volume on snatches of everyday conversations, kindergarten plays, and childhood fears? Like my grandfather, I have forgotten the big things and remembered the little ones. There is probably coming a day when I will forget the names of my two children and remember with clarity Mickey Mantle's statistics in 1957.

One boyhood memory is surprisingly vivid. I was eleven or twelve years old and visiting my two cousins in a small South Texas town. It was a summer Sunday evening, and we were in a Training Union class at the First Baptist Church. Small wooden chairs were arranged in rows in the front half of the upstairs classroom. We had arrived before the teacher, and my cousins introduced me to a handful of children. Then, to properly impress her friends, one cousin added a special word about my piety. "He reads the Bible three times a day," she said with pride.

"Is that true?" her friends asked with new respect.

I shook my head in the affirmative. "Well, almost every day," I said. I felt embarrassed about the disclosure but smug too. I was glad I had been set apart as a serious Christian.

I'm not sure why Time has turned up the volume on that particular memory tape. It may have no more significance than some of the other tapes that periodically "click on" in my head, such as the one about the free pancake breakfast served that clear, icy morning under a gigantic tent on the parking lot of Epps' Grocery Store. Time may be just a mischievous prankster turning knobs on a whim.

But Memory may be more precise than we suspect. The knobs may be methodically controlled by something (or Someone) more careful than Chance. My grandfather may remember the purchase of the forty acres of land because that was a highlight of his life, a dream fulfilled. At least in my own case, I suspect that incident twenty-five years ago in the upstairs classroom is loud in my head for a very good reason. Even then, that tape reminds me, I wanted to be a "serious Christian."

It is a distinction I still crave. Memory could well be my best friend and most honest advisor, whispering clues to my real identity. If I listen closely enough, I may discover who I am and who I've always been.

This much I know: serious faith has been my trademark since childhood. At the age of seven I made my "profession of faith" in Christ at a Baptist church in northwest Houston and was baptized. The script that has unfolded since that decision, Memory tells me, has been a predictable one. My script was titled "Dedicated Disciple," and I have followed it with scarcely a slip.

What my cousin gloated about was true: I *did* read the Bible three times a day as a child. Even as a teenager, I faithfully read my Bible every day and whenever I was facing a pressure situation. The Bible became my good luck charm. Secure in the knowledge that I had claimed God's promises, I marched into school tests, football games, neighborhood skirmishes, and other assorted challenges with as much courage as possible for a timid youngster.

Two Old Testament verses became my favorites. The first was Deuteronomy 31:6: "Be strong and courageous. Do not be afraid or terrified because of them, for the Lord your God goes with you; he will never leave you nor forsake you." The other, Psalm 31:24: "Be strong and take heart, all you who hope in the LORD."

Even though I shortly had those verses memorized, I always read them from the Bible. There was something about taking the Book in hand that made the ritual more significant. I would scurry into my bedroom before a Little League baseball game, open my Bible, and read again those two promises. Then, bolstered by God's words of encouragement, I knew I could step into the batter's box with confidence.

All of the verses I claimed in my youth had to do with the strength God gives and the foolishness of worry. I often felt insecure and afraid, but armed with the biblical pebbles, I trusted I could slay the giants that confronted me.

The script continued to unfold predictably. I was leader of a Bible study group on my high school campus, faithful attender of all our church's activities, and abstainer from all teenage vices. While my teammates on the football team dabbled in sex, drink, and foul language, I went merrily and piously on my way, refusing even to go to the senior prom because it involved dancing. Amazingly, I was voted outstanding senior boy, but as I look back, the award was by vote of the faculty, not the student body. At least the adults in my world appreciated my walk down the straight-and-narrow way!

After high school I enrolled in the largest Baptist university in the world. One experience I had my freshman year is another of those "loud tapes" that reminds me of my long yearning to be a serious Christian.

Someone gave me a "witnessing button" that year. It was just a little lapel button—yellow with a red maze on it. The button was to serve as an opening for evangelistic witnessing. When a curious person asked about it, the wearer was then to tell how Christ can lead a person out of the mystifying maze of life.

That button made me miserable for weeks. I was afraid to wear it because I knew some inquisitive soul would ask me about it and I would then have to unleash my personal testimony. Every time I opened my jewelry box, the maze-button scoffed at me and accused me of bashful faith. Finally, to ease my guilt, I pinned the button on my shirt and put a sweater over it. I comforted myself that I did, indeed, have the nerve to witness, but was assured at the same time that no one would ever ask me about my peculiar button.

My friend Memory is again telling me something. I have wanted to be a bold Christian most of my life, but my temperament resists. Part of me wants to shout a testimony, but another part wants to leave people alone. Something in me says, "Go ye into all the world," and something else says, "Don't cast your personal pearls before swine." And that same battle rages to this day.

Just before my junior year in college, I knelt one evening by my bed and told God I would preach his Word. There were no dramatic incidents that led to the decision, just a growing awareness that I would be most useful in that capacity. I changed my major to religion and became a ministerial student. The following year I graduated with a Bachelor of Arts Degree.

The summer after graduation I married a devout Christian girl, and we moved to Fort Worth, Texas, where I enrolled in the largest Baptist seminary in the world. I also became pastor of a country church that year. Every weekend for over two years, Sherry and I drove the 350-mile round trip to the booming burg of Andice where forty or fifty kindhearted folks gathered every Sunday to endure my homiletic gems.

After seminary, it was on to a children's home where I served for two-and-a-half years as chaplain and then to the pastorate of a suburban church outside Houston where we have been ever since. Through the years our family has grown to four members, and our church has become a moderate-sized congregation of middle-class professionals. My faith has grown and deepened, but I am still struggling with what it means to follow Christ—thirty years after my baptism. I am still trying to define for myself what it means to be a "serious Christian."

When I first decided to try my hand at writing and looked deep inside for something to say, I was not surprised at what surfaced. The book *A Matter of Choice*, published by my denomination's press, had this explanatory "blurb" on the cover: "A Handbook for Those Who Don't Want to Be Squeezed in by the World." Based on Romans 12:2 ("Do not conform any longer to the pattern of this world, but be transformed by the renewing of your mind"), the book was, in short, a handbook for serious Christians.

Looking back on all of these experiences—claiming God's promises during private sessions in the bedroom, shunning the senior prom, witnessing with a button, attending the denominational schools, marrying the Christian girl, writing the book on biblical nonconformity—reminds me again of my true identity. Each of these memories is really saying the same thing: "Your lifelong quest has been to please God, to be the epitome of the true believer."

But as I look back on the journey, there is a softer, subtler melody that has dogged me too. I have always hungered for joy. Even while learning to march to the gospel commands, I wanted also to dance.

As I write these words at the desk in my study, I can see the books I've bought over the years on the shelves beside me. Those books represent stops on the way of faith, spiritual passages I've been through. But all along the way, those books tell me, there has been a desire for joy. *The Key to Triumphant Living, Ask Me to Dance, Life More Abundant, Jesus Makes*

Me Laugh, That Elusive Thing Called Joy, Come to the Party, To a Dancing God—these and dozens of the other books bear silent testimony to my mostly unvoiced longing. Any discerning person rummaging through the books on my shelves would arrive at this conclusion: Here is a Christian man hungry for happiness.

A passage from one of these books perfectly expresses my hunger:

> If I had my life to live over, I'd try to make more mistakes next time. I would relax, I would limber up, I would be sillier than I have been this trip. I know of very few things I would take seriously. I would be less hygienic. I would take more chances. I would take more trips. I would climb more mountains, swim more rivers, and watch more sunsets. I would eat more ice cream. I would have actual troubles and fewer imaginary ones.
>
> You see, I am one of those people who lives prophylactically and sensibly and sanely, hour after hour, day after day. Oh, I have had my moments and, if I had it to do over again, I'd have nothing else. Just moments, one after another, instead of living so many years ahead of each day. I have been one of those people who never go anywhere without a thermometer, a hot water bottle, a gargle, a raincoat, and a parachute. If I had it to do over again, I would go places and do things and travel lighter than I have.
>
> If I had my life to live over again, I would start barefooted earlier in the spring and stay that way later in the fall. I would play hooky more. I wouldn't make such good grades except by accident. I would ride on more merry-go-rounds. I would pick more daisies.[1]

That is a quote from an anonymous friar in a Nebraska monastery, used by John Killinger in his book *Bread for the Wilderness, Wine for the Journey*. But I could have written those words too. The friar and I are kindred spirits. I too have lived "sensibly and sanely" all of my days. Only now, like my brother in the monastery, I'm beginning to wonder why.

I now realize that my model for life has been the apostle Paul, not Jesus Christ. At least not the Jesus who told earthy stories, went to festive parties, and hung out with the wrong crowd. Not the Jesus who was accused of being a glutton and a winebibber. I have had little to do with that Jesus.

Paul has been my man—always heavy on his feet, intense even in prison, chiding backsliders, exhorting the downtrodden, marching from place to place bearing the gospel, physically suffering for his faith. Paul, the diligent crusader, has been my lord, and he has both challenged and intimidated me.

I cannot imagine Paul cracking a bawdy joke or taking a nap in a hammock or spending a whole day fishing in his favorite stream. No, my impression of Paul is that of the serious Christian, Bible in hand, always pressing and pushing for Christ. Who has time for fishing, I hear him say, when the souls of men are in the balance?

Because I am the apostle's disciple, I have found myself with nagging pangs of guilt when I picnic in the park or spend the day reading a novel. How can a man of God fritter away his life like that? Why can't I be committed like Paul? Another book on the shelf says it plainly: *When I Relax I Feel Guilty.*

Edna Hong, in her book *The Downward Ascent*, says, "The Word sometimes tolls like a funeral bell in my mind and sometimes does a ragtime jig."[2] I suppose the thrust of this entire chapter can be summed up like this: I have cultivated an ear for the Word as funeral bell, but I have longed to hear the ragtime jig.

Is that longing justified? Should a serious Christian want ecstasy? Or is that hunger for joy just accommodation to a culture that measures everything by consumer satisfaction? Is my desire to dance a selfish one? Does Christ want me committed or content? What is his will for me—the sword of the crusader or the peace that passes all understanding?

Let me try next to shape an answer to those questions.

2.

Peace or a Sword?

Anyone who claims the Bible is an easy book to understand just doesn't understand it. While we would like to make it a "spiritual yellow pages" with easy answers to hard questions, careful study reveals otherwise. If we go to Scripture with our pressing questions about joy, we do not get the straightforward response we want. Approach the Holy Word with this question—Does God want me content or crucified?—and it will give you a vague, even contradictory answer.

Look at the words of Jesus in the Gospels, and you can make a case either way. Once he said, "Do not suppose that I have come to bring peace to the earth. I did not come to bring peace, but a sword" (Matt 10:34). His is the way of the sword, of warfare with unseen principalities and powers. But that same Jesus later comforted his disciples with these words: "Peace I leave with you; my peace I give to you. I do not give to you as the world gives. Do not let your hearts be troubled and do not be afraid" (John 14:27). His is also the way of comfort and rest. So which is it: peace or a sword? The two statements seem to be in conflict.

On another occasion Jesus said to his disciples, "If anyone would come after me, he must deny himself and take up his cross and follow me. For whoever wants to save his life will lose it, but whoever loses his life for me will find it" (Matt 16:24-25). Obviously, his way is a hard way of denial, sacrifice, and even death. But he also said to his followers, "Come to me, all you who are weary and burdened, and I will give you rest. Take my yoke upon you and learn from me, for I am gentle and humble in heart, and you will find rest for your souls. For my yoke is easy and my burden is light" (Matt 11:28-30). His way is also one of rest, relaxation, and lifted burdens. So which yoke shall we carry: the heavy one of self-denial or the light one of rest?

E. B. White, the great essayist, once wrote, "If the world were merely seductive, that would be easy. If it were merely challenging, that would be no problem, but I arise in the morning torn between a desire to improve (or save) the world and a desire to enjoy (or savor) the world. This makes it hard to plan the day."[1] That is our dilemma too. To save or savor—that is our question. And Jesus seems to speak out of both sides of his mouth. How can we handle the seeming contradiction of his words?

The tension can be approached two ways. The first way is to let the contradiction stand, to recognize that Jesus is more mysterious than we like to admit. We want him to be accurate and consistent like a mathematician, but the Gospel writers present him as unpredictable and enigmatic like One from Somewhere Else. Perhaps the best, most honest way to handle the tension in his words is not to handle them at all, but to let them rattle against our logic until we remember just who he is: God-Man, the ultimate contradiction.

My mind does not sit easy with that though. I am a product of the scientific age, and contradiction is rough sandpaper in my head. I want to resolve the tension and make Christ's words come out even, like a balanced equation.

So I turn to the second way of handling the contradiction: He said precisely what was needed in different settings. At one point he called for commitment because the need was for discipline and backbone. Another time he spoke rejuvenating words of comfort because the need was relaxation and cheer. To put it another way, he disturbed the comfortable and comforted the disturbed.

Checking the context of the verses in question bears out this idea. When he said he came to bring a sword and not peace, Christ was addressing his disciples before sending them on an evangelistic mission. They were going out as "sheep in the midst of wolves" and needed strong commitment to make the journey. Half-hearted, "laid back" faith would not suffice. They needed militant allegiance and the sword of radical devotion. Those disciples had to deny self, turn their backs on their families, and take up the cross of sacrifice if they were going to be fit travelers. So Jesus spoke the needed word: "I did not come to bring peace, but a sword."

The passage where he promises peace to those same men has a completely different setting. The shadow of the cross looms in the background of this passage. Christ was telling his friends of his coming crucifixion and giving them hope and comfort. Their dreams of a messianic kingdom shattered, they desperately needed some good news, some assurance that they would be able to survive the coming tragedy, some promise that would still their pounding hearts. So Jesus spoke the needed word: "Peace I leave with you; my peace I give you."

The seeming contradiction vanishes when we see the setting of Christ's words. When his disciples were comfortable, he said disturbing things to prepare them for the hostility of an evil world. When they were disturbed about the news of his death, he said comforting things to bandage their wounded spirits. Sometimes peace, and sometimes a sword—his necessary word depended upon the circumstances.

When you think about Christ's dealings with people in the Gospels, you can repeatedly see him determine each person's pressing need. He did not approach all people the same way, prescribe the same remedy for all ills, offer mass therapy for people, or utter a standard slogan to plug into every life. Christ saw every person he related to as an individual with special needs.

He told the young ruler, possessed by his possessions, to sell all and give the money to the poor. He told Nicodemus, proud of his Jewish birthright, to be born again and start over from scratch. He spoke to the Samaritan woman at the well, whose sexual flightiness signaled a thirst for meaning, of new and living water. To the paralytic lowered through the roof and the woman caught in adultery, Christ offered words of unconditional forgiveness. Sometimes he just healed a sick person and said nothing about spiritual matters. He was loving to the outcasts and sinners, and shockingly harsh with the scribes and Pharisees. Everyone Jesus met got personal treatment as the Great Physician dispensed different medicine for different diseases.

When the ailment was flippant, casual living, Jesus prescribed denying self, taking up a cross, picking up a sword. When the ailment was exhaustion or despondency, he talked of easy yokes, light burdens, a legacy of peace. And both words, as contradictory as they sound, are good news. When you are floundering in indecision or selfishness, Christ's call to commitment is sweet music. And when you are run-down or burned-out, his invitation to rest, his insistence that you dump all of your misery on him, is the best news imaginable.

Our task is to determine which is the pressing word for *us*. We must decide which is our malady: the spiritual apathy that needs strident orders or the spiritual weariness that can be cured only by a heavy dose of relaxation and joy.

Many people need the former. Aimlessness is a national plague. Video games, packaged vacations, extramarital affairs, expensive trinkets, and silly movies are the only medicines many in our society ever take to try to heal a restless spirit. The word of commitment to Christ needs to be sounded in such a world. Those prophetic voices calling people out of the quicksand of Self are doing them a great favor. They are offering an alternative to despair. When your prime goal in life is to increase your score at the video arcade, the demands of a loving Lord to build a kingdom sound awfully good. When you are futilely jogging in place, the command to march is good news.

But millions of people—especially Christian people—need the word of peace. Look at the faces in the pews next Sunday morning, and you will come to believe that John 10:10 is an unfulfilled prophecy: "I am come that they might have life, and that they might have it more abundantly" (KJV). Those faithful people know little about abundant living. They know much of commitment, but they are ignorant of joy.

Sadly, for most of those in this second group, the gospel has lost its power to evoke any response. They cannot be gladdened by it because they can no longer hear it. The Good News, for them, is neither good nor news.

It is not good because they see it as an exacting taskmaster. They have wept in repentance, tithed, studied Bible lessons, visited the sick, sung in cantatas, verbally witnessed for their Lord, and prayed without ceasing. But they have not been able to please the gospel taskmaster who sees all of their righteousness as filthy rags. Try as they might to pay up, the message they always hear is: "Rent demanded."

And the gospel is no longer news to them either. Henri Nouwen's observation is painfully accurate:

> Practically nobody listens to a sermon with the expectation of hearing something they did not already know. They have heard about Jesus—His disciples, His savings, His miracles, His death and resurrection—at home, in kindergarten, in grade school, in high school, and in college so often and in so many different ways and forms that the last thing they expect to come from the pulpit is any news. And the core of the Gospel—"You must love the Lord your God with all your heart, with all your soul, and with all your mind and you must love your neighbor as yourself"—has been repeated so often and so persistently that it has lost, for the majority of people, even the slightest possibility of evoking any response.[2]

Honestly, who comes to church anymore expecting to be surprised by God's Word? Its familiarity has bred, if not contempt, at least indifference in us. Who, when the preacher rises to proclaim that Word, leans forward in anticipation of something outlandish and wild? Our typical response is to shift our minds onto "autopilot" and take a thirty-minute snooze. After all, we've heard it all before.

When this happens, Christianity becomes a boring attempt to remember old lines and rehearse old steps. Our relationship to Christ becomes stale and uneventful. And usually the only antidote we know is to pray more, give more, and do more. Ironically, we fight exhaustion with activity and just make ourselves more exhausted.

This brand of spirituality—call it the Faithful-but-Joyless Kind— eventually produces a certain kind of person. Robert Capon, through the character Gertrude Schlosskaese in his book *Between Noon and Three*, describes this person well:

> When I look at my middle-aged children, I feel sad. It seems to me that instead of becoming freer as they've gotten older, they've gotten more and more afraid of failure—to the point where they don't feel they can risk anything. And I wonder if that isn't due to the way they were raised—all the emphasis we put on being acceptable, all the fear of making mistakes we drummed into them. I see them passing on the same fear. They're wonderful people, successful and very responsible. But they're so depress- ingly conventional, so tight, so tense. Sometimes I think I must be turning into a swinger. I was so afraid of their non-conformity when they were young, now it's their very conformity that frightens me. And the sad part is they don't even seem to be happy in their successes; they seem to be trapped by them.
>
> ...Grace really does have to be given more attention. If it isn't, all we'll see is grown people who are more afraid than children—and who have to hide from their fear in work, or drink, or a lot of other things that, as they use them, are just—well, joyless.[3]

Though it hurts to admit it, those words describe most of us who have been dedicated Christians for years. This is who we are: conventional, tight, tense, successful, responsible, trapped, joyless. It makes us wince to confess it, but confession will hopefully be the beginning of change.

Most books and sermons are aimed at the group needing more zeal, commitment, and guidance. But those books and sermons become Bad News when they reach the wrong crowd. Committed people chafe under the commands for more commitment. Weary folks grow angry or depressed when urged to "do more for Jesus." The last thing in the world some dedi- cated Christians need to hear is that their problems stem from a lack of dedication. Imagine Christ saying to the disconsolate disciples before his death, "I did not come to bring peace, but a sword." What comfort is there in that when your world is about to collapse?

This book is aimed at the faithful-joyless crowd, the deeply committed followers of Christ whose earnest, but silent plea echoes David's: "Restore to me the joy of your salvation" (Ps 51:12). Though we are mostly quiet about our plight, I think our numbers are legion.

If an honest survey of our souls reveals a dry, dusty spirit thirsty for laughter and freedom and relaxation, we have determined our agenda. And we need not feel guilty for following the agenda our spirit sets. Our first priority is to recover our joy. In truth, if we don't recover our joy, we will soon have trouble summoning discipline or worshiping or fighting off temptation. Joy is the fuel that propels us to serve God, and nobody goes far without the motivation only joy can give.

There will perhaps come a time when our inventory reveals a lax, lukewarm spirituality. When that happens, honesty demands that we come under the influence of all of those hard, commitment, judgment parts of Scripture. At times, we are the disciples embarking on the preaching mission, and we need to hear that Jesus came not to bring peace, but a sword.

But for now, suspend those sayings. Let them find another audience. You and I need joy. We need to be more foolish, to loosen up, to join the friar in riding merry-go-rounds and picking daisies, to let the Good News really get hold of us. We need "Peace I give you" and "Come to me, all you who are weary and burdened" and "Those who hope in the Lord will renew their strength." We need "Thou wilt keep him in perfect peace whose mind is stayed on thee" (KJV) and "Therefore, there is now no condemnation for those who are in Christ Jesus" and "Stand fast therefore in the liberty wherewith Christ hath made us free" (KJV).

For now, forget about marching. God is asking you to dance.

3.
The Crucial Confession

Let me put on my soothsayer's hat and try to peek into your soul. I may know more about you than you realize.

- You are a model of faith and virtue, and those in your family and church hold you in high esteem.
- You occasionally have sexual fantasies and are extremely grateful that no one can see the "movies" that run through your head.
- You have had secret doubts about God and wish he were more audible and visible.
- You honestly do not feel like a "responsible adult" and sometimes feel overwhelmed by life.
- You have one fear—your children will be killed in an accident or you will contract a terrible disease or you will lose your job—that haunts you regularly.
- You do not feel as close to people as you would like. Lack of intimacy is a problem.
- You have read the Bible for years and believe it to be God's Word, but you also feel perplexed and guilty that most of it seems out of touch with your life.
- You have periodic bouts with depression that you hide from even your closest friends—even though you claim your trust in God has long given you meaning and hope.
- You have one nagging skeleton in your closet that will not grant you peace. It rattles occasionally, making you feel fresh guilt over an old crime.
- You do not have as much joy in your life as you wish.
- You have become an expert at hiding your true beliefs and feelings and frequently feel the tension that comes from "putting up a front."

If my predictions are anywhere near accurate, they only confirm what you already know but are hesitant to admit: You are a flawed human being who doesn't "have it all together." To put it in blunt, biblical terms: You are a sinner who has fallen far short of the glory of God.

But ironically, that admission leads to joy. Admit your sin and struggle, and you take a giant step toward abundant living. Steadfastly maintain personal purity and innocence, and you stay trapped in joylessness.

The church has long revered Peter's confession at Caesarea Philippi: "You are the Christ, the Son of the living God" (Matt 16:16). Justifiably, that statement has been called the Great Confession. All people need to make that proclamation of faith.

But it is time the church gave attention to the confession of Paul and Barnabas at Lystra as well: "We also are men of like passions with you" (Acts 14:15, KJV). That is probably life's second greatest confession. When the people of Lystra wanted to call them gods, Paul and Barnabas had the good sense to confess their humanity. And that confession is crucial to joy! If the Caesarean confession is the key to finding heaven, the Lystra confession is the key to finding joy. Admitting our humanity is more important than we realize.

It is important for two reasons. First, confessing our humanity opens the door to God's forgiveness, and second, it opens the door to mutuality, or kinship, with people. Until we make this crucial confession, we cut ourselves off from both divine and human love.

We cut ourselves off from God's love because we see no need of his forgiveness. At first glance, it seems admirable to be morally perfect, to adopt a stance of righteous piety—until you realize how easily that translates into never needing forgiveness. The harlot, for all her depravity, will have more joy than the sanctimonious Pharisee who feels guiltless. Because she has been absolved of obvious sin, she at least knows the wonder of grace. The Pharisee only knows the tedium of the law. His plight is the one all morally upright people face: "But whoever has been forgiven little loves little" (Luke 7:47).

Why do you suppose Jesus saved his harshest words for the religious men of his day? They were sincere, reputable, moral men, but Christ scalded them with bitter denunciation. I think he dealt with them so severely because they needed to be confronted with the reality of their sin. As long as they saw themselves as righteous and whole, they had no need of a Physician and no need of grace. Jesus came not to call the righteous, but sinners, so the scribes and Pharisees had no use for him. Why would a sinless keeper-of-the-law need a Savior?

Those religious leaders were playing a devastating game—the Sinless-and-Perfect Game. Anyone who plays it is guaranteed a life of respectable, religious misery. All you have to do to play the game is deny your guilt. March against pornographers but ignore your own lust. Preach and teach against materialism but never recognize that you are trapped in it too. Fail to notice that your tirades against spiritual apathy hide your own lack of commitment. Chastise doubters and ignore the fact that you too have doubts. In essence, turn your focus on the sins of the outer world so you never have to face the sins of your inner world. Judge others so you never have to judge yourself.

Several years ago, I attended a meeting of church staff members to plan a summer camp for the teenagers in our churches. A dispute arose over whether or not the boys and girls should swim together at camp. One man in particular was vocal in opposition to the mixed swimming idea. He threatened not to bring the young people from his church if we allowed mixed swimming. Since he was the only one adamant about separate swimming times, though, we voted to let the sexes swim together. And true to his threat, he and his young people boycotted camp that summer.

The next year when we convened to plan camp, the man was absent. It was casually mentioned that he no longer served on the staff of the church. Later I learned why. He had had an affair with a woman in the church and had been dismissed from his position.

The picture then became clear. His opposition to the teenagers swimming together was a reflection of his own inner battle. He was projecting *his* lust onto them. His anger at the notion of mixed swimming was actually misplaced anger that should have been directed at himself. In hurling stones at potentially promiscuous teens, he was avoiding having to throw them at his own promiscuity.

And I can't throw too many rocks at him either. We are all guilty of his crime. We all project our personal sins onto others so we don't have to deal with them. We would like to think we are sinless and perfect so we can yell righteous condemnation at our evil comrades. But the man at the camp meeting is an unforgettable reminder to me that failing to face up to who we really are is, itself, evil and destructive. One whose spirituality is built on self-deception has a foundation made of sand.

To be sure, the Sinless-and-Perfect Game does have its rewards. It will get you a distorted sort of esteem, but esteem nonetheless. Neighbors will call you righteous. Your church will laud your circumspect life. Your children will take your cue and keep the commandments. But you will be joyless because, like the New Testament religious leaders, you will be detached from forgiveness.

Am I suggesting that we carouse, commit adultery, or cheat on our income tax so that we can be forgiven and then fully appreciate grace? Not at all. A far more competent theologian than I has addressed the subject of presuming on grace. "Shall we go on sinning so that grace may increase?" (Rom 6:1), he asked. And his answer was pointed: "By no means!" (Rom 6:2). To use the grace of God as license to do wrong is, of course, a perversion of the gospel message. Presuming on grace, Paul said, is a tell-tale sign we don't have grace in us at all. Anyone who cheats on God just because he is merciful has an obviously inadequate relationship with him.

But the point is we don't use grace as a ticket for future sin; we embrace it as our only hope for current sin. Carousing, adultery, and income tax evasion are not our real problems anyway. Even if those things are present in our lives, they are but the visible outcroppings of a much more pervasive iceberg. Our real sin is the misshapen, misguided Self we are, a Self that seeks its own good at all costs, a Self so twisted it is beyond human repair. We do everything in our power to channel our Self toward God but finally despair and fall back on God's incredible grace.

Paul too fought this losing battle with Self. In Romans 7 he detailed the awful war that raged within him. He did what he knew was sin, he said, and did not do what he knew was righteous. He was, in his own words, a "wretched man" and terribly tormented. But where did this river of anguish sweep him? Right into the ocean of grace: "There is therefore now no condemnation to them which are in Christ Jesus, who walk not after the flesh, but after the Spirit. For the law of the Spirit of life in Christ Jesus hath made me free from the law of sin and death" (Rom 8:1-2 KJV).

For all of his sin—or because of all of his sin—Paul saw the need to splash in God's grace. Bathing in his own righteousness only left him dirty and hopeless. But the scribes and Pharisees, because of their respectability, never made it to the ocean of grace. Jesus tried to move them toward it, but they never made it. Their game was Sinless-and-Perfect, and they would not change. They never knew that the Sinful-and-Forgiven Game is much more fun to play.

If we follow them and opt for Sinless-and-Perfect, our prime goal is to prove to others how good we are. In reality, the object of the game is to impress people with our goodness. Maintaining a spotless reputation assumes top priority in our dealings with others.

If, on the other hand, we choose to play Sinful-and-Forgiven, our prime concern is to reflect how good *God* is. We are free to be human, to let loose of our stilted piety, to play the fool, and in Martin Luther's packed phrase, to "sin boldly." The person who plays Sinful-and-Forgiven is free to romp through life; and the Sinless-and-Perfect one must always tiptoe.

I remember when I first heard of a local church called The Church of the Holy Innocents. If one has to be holy and innocent to enter her doors, I thought, attendance will be rather slim! But most of us persist in trying to project that image to the world. We committed Christians have much of the Pharisee in us. And in trying to maintain our holiness and innocence, we tragically cut off God's forgiveness. Only when we tire of treading water in our own righteousness will we ever be carried to the ocean of God's grace, a grace that turns joyless perfectionists into joyful sinners.

But our insistence on being "Christian" and above the sins and temptations of the world has a second devastating result as well. Not only does it detach us from grace, it also ruins our chance for intimacy with others.

Do you really think the Pharisee had any close friends? Do you think the common man rushed to him to swap yarns or talk theology or grieve when the baby died? I think not. The Pharisee, for all of his good intentions, had erected a barrier around himself. It was a barrier made of fine materials—prayer, Scripture, fasting, public worship, and righteous deeds—but a barrier nonetheless.

In our desire to be "spiritual," we too can erect a similar barrier, and the people around us just cannot make contact with us. Bruce Lockerbie writes about this problem in his book *The Timeless Moment*:

> One of the paradoxes of our experiences as Christians wishing to serve God is this: The more "spiritual" we become, the less effective seems to be our witness among those who know nothing but the tedium of secular existence. On the other hand, the more we know of physical labor and perspiration, comradeship and disappointment, love and loss; the closer we grow to the soil and to those soiled by life's vicissitudes; the deeper we probe the recesses of human fear and aspiration—in short, the greater our joy both in being human and in knowing who made us so—then and only then are we enough like Christ himself to perceive how best to devote our gift to his glory.[1]

Think for a moment about your own relationships. When you want to celebrate, who do you invite to join you? When life grows stale, where do you go? When you need a listening ear, to whom do you turn? Chances are, you turn to an ordinary, down-to-earth person, someone who has been touched by the hurt and gladness of life, someone who is real and who grants you the liberty to be yourself. The truth is, very few of us get along well with Superman. In our joys and sorrows, we don't need a super-spiritual saint with no flaws. We need a cracked, earthen pot (2 Cor 4:7), to use Paul's terminology, who can sit where we sit and relate to our feelings.

I think there is a crying need in the church today for cracked pots (not crackpots—the church has enough of those already!) who will dare to be fully human and fully Christian. Why are we evangelical Christians so tight and tense and respectable? Why are we so "hung up" on words and doctrines and impeccable credentials? Why can't we just be ordinary people who have been called out by Christ to love others?

The new Christian Reformation needs to be an uprising of eccentrics, a resurgence of people obstinate in their humanity and individualism. The church, for too long, has been mass-producing believers. Kierkegaard once said, "The ideal Christian is happily married, looks like a cheerful grocer, and is respected by his neighbors."[2] We have plenty of cheerful grocers, predictable preachers, and orthodox lay people now. We have more than enough assembly line saints who all talk the same language and live by the same code. We are woefully short of eccentrics, though. We need people who are proud of their particularity, people who, in boldly living the difference to which they have been called, encourage others to do the same.

I guess we just need people like Jesus who, in his freedom, so unsettled the status quo. He was a real human and, unlike the religious elite, was attractive and approachable. He went to parties, told good tales, fished with friends, wept in grief, agonized in Gethsemane, and loved common folks. Jesus, though he was God's Son, was fully human, and everywhere he roamed, people reached out to touch him and longed to be near him.

But it seems we "spiritual" people cannot be fully human. In masking our humanity, we destroy our best chance for witness to a human world. Unlike our Lord, our spirituality severs our kinship with ordinary people. Karl Olsson writes:

> Nowhere does our independence of God glow so fiercely as in
> our goodness. When our desire for perfection drives us into moral

scrupulousness or even into self-effacing benevolence, we feel with Milton's Eve "divinity within us breeding wings."

This is why ordinary people feel more uneasy about saints, martyrs, and heroes than about sinners, traitors, and cowards. It is very trying to have a saint in for dinner, especially a saint working on being more saintly. Our guilt may cause us to raise pedestals for spiritual giants and prayer warriors, but we would rather have them gracing our sanctuaries than invading our houses.[3]

Olsson is right. A saint in the sanctuary is tolerable, and even admirable. A saint at the supper table is insufferable.

Our willingness to live our humanity—to admit our doubts, to laugh and cry, to confess our inadequacy, to acknowledge we have no answer to life's mysteries—is crucial to our human relationships. We must be truthful, for no legitimate faith and no enriching relationship can be constructed of falsehood.

Of course I know of the flighty "sharing"so popular in encounter groups. I know of the blabbing of one's innermost self to strangers that some people think is "getting real" and "being honest." I have sat through embarrassing "sharing and testimony" times in church done under the guise of fostering intimacy among the believers. But those things are cheap caricatures of what we all crave—for our spirit to touch another person's spirit in a way that lets us know and be known.

As bad as these "sharing" sessions are, though, they are preferable to the other extreme. The Pharisees' way of "holy and innocent" is worse because it is a blatant lie. Never admitting or expressing our humanity will always repel others because they will see through our game. And we will reap the miserable existence of the lonesome liar, the one George Sheehan describes all too well: "The true loneliness, then, is me seeing that nothing I do is true. Me and this inner emptiness, me and the abyss, me and the false me I am with other people, me being what I do, what I accomplish, the clever things I say. Me and that living of a lie, a long, lonely lifetime lie."[4]

Another book on the shelf beside me bears the title *For God's Sake, Be Human*. That book deserves a sequel, though: *For Others' Sake, Be Human*. For others' sake, we must never become spiritual elitists, isolated from music, sports, jokes, movies, and books. For others' sake, we must keep our feet on the ground. For others' sake, we must be true to the difference to which we have been called. For others' sake, we must confess with Paul and Barnabas, "We also are men of like passions with you."

I fear Edna Hong alludes to many of us "good Christians" in a piece she has written:

> Neither radiant saints nor flagrant sinners, many brought-up Chris-
> tians drift along horizontally, never recognizing their true natures, never
> discovering their sins, and never being surprised by grace. Meeting their
> own standards of goodness and morality, tucked up in their cozy over-
> simplifications, they talk as if the Christian community, the Christian
> congregation, the Christian family, the Christian individual—really and
> truly Christian, that is—have no problems whatsoever with evil and
> suffering in the world or with evil and suffering within themselves. As
> if they themselves, being Christian, never felt the pangs of loneliness,
> confusion, doubt, anguish of mind and spirit. As if to admit that they
> had these feelings occasionally were to admit that they were not true or
> twice-born Christians.[5]

The Good News is that we can admit these feelings—indeed, that we must admit them. Until we do, we will know nothing of the divine forgive-ness that makes us "love much." And we will isolate ourselves from those people who just need "a person of like passions" to know and love them.

The toughest battle you will ever have to fight is the battle to be your-self, to live your destiny and celebrate your humanity. But since the prizes are an awareness of God's grace and kinship with others, it is a battle well worth fighting.

4.

Getting the Horse
Back Before the Cart

Grace is the first word in the Christian experience. Our relationship to God begins with his unbelievable, unwarranted acceptance of us: "For it is by grace you have been saved, through faith—and this not from yourselves, it is the gift of God" (Eph 2:8).

Becoming Christian means we step into the healing flow of God's grace and then spend the rest of our days singing about it. Because a grace-full God is the initiator of the relationship, we can admit our wrongs, claim our humanity, and know that nothing "will be able to separate us from the love of God that is in Christ Jesus our Lord" (Rom 8:39).

Our part, as unbelievable as it sounds, is only to keep our lives open to his love. As Capon puts it, "The life of grace is the life of a cripple on an escalator: as far as being able to walk is concerned, he is simply dead; there is nothing for him to do. But then he doesn't need to do anything, because the divine Floorwalker has kindly put him on the eternally moving staircase of Jesus—and up he goes."[1]

Grace, however, is also the first word we Christians forget. Glad acceptance of grace nearly always degenerates into burdensome, bootstrap religion. Perhaps the news of free salvation is too good to believe. Perhaps our work-your-way-up-the-ladder-of-success culture has us in its deadly clutches. Perhaps the law, for all of its demands, is more tolerable than the frightening freedom grace gives us. Whatever the reason, there is a strange inclination in the faithful to shun grace and start crawling up the escalator. To use Paul's phrase to the Galatian Christians, we inevitably "fall away from grace."

This abandoning of grace is the prime reason so many Christians are miserable. Leave grace out of the gospel pie, and it is absolutely unpalatable. Tasting it makes for sour, sad saints.

Can you imagine a hamburger without the patty? A cake without sugar? A Thanksgiving feast without the turkey? In each case the one flavorful ingredient is absent, and without it the whole enterprise goes down the drain. When we "fall away from grace," the Bible loses its intrigue and becomes a dull compilation of impossible divine edicts. Our relationship to God becomes that strenuous, life-draining struggle up the escalator of morality and religious deeds.

Yet the pie can be incredibly delicious. The way to taste it fresh again is to remember the difference between a transaction and a celebration.

A transaction is a piece of business done to earn a payment or reward. You write the check to buy the week's groceries, and the grocer dutifully takes your check and sacks your goods; a transaction has been completed. You have done your part, and the grocery store has done its part.

A celebration, on the other hand, is just that: spontaneous joy and merriment because of some momentous event, festivity because of an undeserved gift. The grocer shows up at your doorstep with a free month's supply of food, so you grill steaks on the pit and invite your neighbors over to tell them of this unbelievable happening. That is celebration. You don't get the groceries in a check transaction; you just open the door and stare in disbelief at the smiling grocer with his load of free goods. Then you can't wait to tell your friends about it.

Our God is either the businesslike grocer demanding payment or the grace-full one who comes with free fare. Our Christianity, in other words, is either transactional or celebrational.

If it is transactional, we do our bits of religious business—prayer, worship, tithing, and all of the other spiritual disciplines—to earn God's favor. We swap personal piety for divine approval. Like the elder brother in the parable of the prodigal, we live above reproach and expect to be rewarded for it.

But we must always be looking over our shoulder to make sure the Father is alert to our goodness. And the bookkeeping becomes tedious. An eye for an eye, a tit for a tat, a good deed for a shower of blessing. Our righteousness is not always what it should be, and even when it is, we know it is really poor currency in God's eyes. There is just no security or joy in a transactional relationship. It lasts only as long as we can keep making notations in our moral ledger.

If our relationship to God is celebrational, though, it will overflow with security and joy. The touchstone of celebrational Christianity is 1 John 4:19: "We love because he first loved us." All of our righteous deeds become not pieces of business to buy divine approval but celebrations of the fact that we already have it. He loved us *first*. He just showed up at the doorstep of our hearts with an eternal load of love, and the only sane response is to spend the rest of our lives thanking him for it and expressing our gratitude by the way we live.

Perhaps a human relationship—that of husband and wife—will best illustrate the distinction. Let us consider two married couples, one with a transactional marriage and one with a celebrational marriage.

The first couple has an unspoken, but nevertheless clearly defined, set of expectations for one another. Though neither partner has ever specifically articulated it, the relationship is the "I will love you if..." brand. The husband has made it clear that his love is conditional: "I will love you if you have sex with me at least twice a week, cook all the meals, balance the checkbook, and keep the kids under reasonable control." The wife has nonverbally communicated her love to him too: "I will love you if you bring home the paycheck, keep your weight under three hundred pounds, and maintain the car and lawn."

This couple firmly believes that marriage is a fifty-fifty proposition. The motto of the relationship is "I will do my part if you will do yours." And everything goes smoothly as long as both spouses make the right transactions. Let one partner fall short of the unwritten agreement, however, and there is big trouble. If the offending spouse errs too long, some divorce lawyer will likely gain a new client.

The second couple has chosen a different model for their relationship. Each partner has communicated to the other this message: "I will love you regardless.... My commitment to you is not dependent on your actions, and I will never entertain the possibility of divorce. For better or worse, I am yours. You are free—free even to take advantage of my unconditional love if you choose."

Their relationship is in no way a fifty-fifty transaction. He is one hundred percent hers, and she is fully his. There is no unspoken agreement by which he earns her love or she earns his. That love is the assumed foundation of everything they do. All of the little kindnesses done for one another—the back massages, the coffee in bed in the morning, the surprise gifts—are done precisely because their love is being celebrated and not purchased. He loves her because she first loved him, and vice versa.

If you protest that this second marriage is a wistful pipe dream, and that no couple you know has such a relationship, I will agree in full. If you insist that unconditional love will not work in a marriage because each partner needs to be accountable to the other, I might reluctantly accede to that too. Very few of us will put up with infidelity or cruelty or even indifference in a marriage. And perhaps we shouldn't.

But I will also insist that people who aim for the goals of this second marriage will have more joy and truer love than is possible in the first marriage. That couple will know wedded bliss unlike any of their friends who are keeping score and trading favors. Because they are secure in their love, the celebrational couple will know the freedom that makes life an adventure. They will know the meaning of grace because they have experienced it personally. Their transactional friends will only know the burden of the unwritten marital law that prescribes an eye for an eye and a tooth for a tooth.

And I will also insist that all of our marriages will be fulfilling and enjoyable to the extent that they are celebrational. The more we move away from the transactional style of conditional love to the celebrational style of unconditional love, the more joy will there be in the relationship. All of us are too steeped in the law to grant our spouses full, Godlike grace, but we certainly should be heading in that direction.

The point of the marriage illustration relates to joy. Whether or not unconditional love is possible in a marriage is really beside the point. What I want you to see is that any transactional relationship is a futile, oppressive exercise. By continually swapping favors the husband and wife will eventually choke all the life out of their love. Only as the couple begins to revel in the love they already have, only as they move from a "works" system to a "grace" system, will the smoldering coals in their marriage flame again. To say it as simply as it can be said: A transactional relationship is a burden; a celebrational relationship is a delight.

Nowhere is this more evident than in our relationship with God. Trying to transact business with him will make us miserable, moral creatures. Celebrating his love, however, will put regular lumps in our throats and persistent mist in our eyes. When we get the order biblically correct—"We love because he first loved us"—joy is the natural result. God's grace is to be the "horse" that pulls the "cart" of glad obedience. If we get the order reversed and let our works try to coax God's grace, we have the cart before the horse and go nowhere.

But this "getting the horse before the cart" is an easy thing to do. Transactional faith is more sensible than celebrational faith. The "works" system is more logical than the "grace" system. From childhood we've been conditioned to believe that we have to work for what we get. So when the grocer shows up with the free groceries, we automatically become suspicious and look for a "catch." Instinctively we protest and reach for the checkbook.

The New Testament says not to bother. The Cross was the transaction that ended all transactions: "For Christ died for sins once for all, the righteous for the unrighteous, to bring you to God" (1 Pet 3:18); "God was in Christ, reconciling the world unto himself" (2 Cor 5:19 KJV); "Therefore, there is now no condemnation to those who are in Christ Jesus" (Rom 8:1). At Calvary, Christ put an end to any notion of negotiating with God. God, amazingly, negotiated the ultimate transaction himself and then signed it with his blood.

All the way through the Old Testament, the interaction between God and man is presented as a series of transactions, as a kind of cosmic chess game where one move calls for another. Man obeys and God blesses. Man sacrifices his lambs, brings his offerings, keeps the commandments, and God responds with his favor. Or man forgets his sacrifices, falls into sin, chases after false gods, and God responds with harsh judgment.

But the New Testament prescribes different rules: "But God demonstrates his own love for us in this: While we were still sinners, Christ died for us" (Rom 5:8). While we were still sinners, it says, God sent his Son to complete the ultimate transaction that put an end to the chess game. Man can make no more effective moves. God has put him in the divine checkmate. God wins the game by losing his only beloved Son and then, unbelievably, sets his captives free. All of those captured by the King are given new life and an invitation to the eternal dance.

Not everyone, of course, believes the news of the divine checkmate. Response to the announcement of the Cross varies from person to person. Paul put the responses in three categories: "But we preach Christ crucified: a stumbling block to Jews and foolishness to Gentiles, but to those whom God has called, both Jews and Greeks, Christ the power of God and the wisdom of God" (1 Cor. 1:23-24). Some see the Cross as a stumbling block. Some see it as utter foolishness. And some dare to see it as the power and wisdom of God. Those three categories still adequately pigeonhole modern man's reaction to the news of Jesus' death.

The "Jews" among us are all of those religious people still trying to transact business with God. The Cross is a stumbling block to them because it interferes with their attempts to buy God's love. They still adhere to the old sacrificial system of religion and regularly bring their morality and piety to the altar to appease God. The modern "Jews" among us refuse to believe the news of the divine checkmate and continue to move pieces in an effort to win. Christendom is full of people for whom the Cross is a stumbling block, people who choose morality over mercy.

The "Greeks" are still among us too—the sophisticated, secular ones who view the Cross as an antiquated myth. To the contemporary "Greeks," the announcement of the divine checkmate is ridiculous. How could the death of a peasant two thousand years ago possibly affect technological man? The "Greeks" among us are still seekers of wisdom and pin their hopes on computers, not crosses.

Then there are those, "both Jews and Greeks," who gladly yield to the checkmate. As absurd as the news of the Cross sounds, some still see it as the pivotal event in all of human history, as the power and wisdom of God, as the consummation of a new covenant of grace. Those in this third category sing with Paul, "I determined not to know any thing among you, save Jesus Christ, and him crucified" (1 Cor 2:2, KJV). They know that the old covenant of burdensome works was nailed to the Cross and that life is now one big celebration of God's grace. They live in gratitude for a salvation not earned, but freely given.

Until we find our way to this third group, the Christian gospel will never be good news to us. The "Jews" will see the gospel as bad news, as a long list of transactions to complete. The "Greeks" seeking wisdom will see the gospel as no news, as religious mumbo-jumbo for the naive and desperate. But the "power and wisdom" bunch will see it as the Good News, as the final squashing of the need for any more transactions. When we understand the Cross for what it is, we're likely to get lumpy-throated and watery-eyed each time we think about it.

Can you imagine being loved that much? Can you believe someone would die for you so that you would no longer have to try to impress God? Can you fathom a life of complete freedom—freedom to be who you are, freedom to love and be loved, freedom to take chances and fail, freedom to live an eternity of celebration? Can you believe God wants you to experience that much joy?

Believe it. That is the message of the Cross, spoken eloquently in silence one dark Friday on a hill called Golgotha. He loved us first! He died for us first! He wanted to end the transactions so the celebration could begin!

Now do you see why they called it Good News?

5.

Cutting Through the Confusion

"Dad, can you help me with my homework?"

Am I the only parent who grimaces when that question comes? It's not that I mind helping, but I've discovered that much of what she is studying I've forgotten. And other things in her sixth-grade textbooks I've never known. Parading my ignorance before her will never be one of my favorite pastimes.

"I'll try," I answer with false bravado. "What do you have to do?"

"Reduce fractions," she yells from her pink bedroom.

Can it be? I wonder. Reducing fractions just like I used to reduce fractions back in the Dark Ages? Have I hit it lucky this time?

I had, indeed. She came with a paper full of old-time fractions, mimeographed in blotty, blue ink, just like the papers I used to do in the sixth grade. She was amazed at my dexterity in handling those cumbersome fractions. I reduced 50/100, 8/12, 25/30, and a string of others without ever putting pencil to paper. When I finished, she looked at my face in disbelief, the way I would look at Einstein's craggy countenance after he'd explained his theory of relativity to me.

I didn't tell her, but she will spend the rest of her education trying to reduce complex things into smaller, simpler tidbits. Reducing fractions is just the beginning. An algebra teacher in the not-too-distant future will have her struggling with a clothesline of x's and y's, and she'll have to factor the equation to its simplest form. A chemistry teacher will assign her the task of breaking down complicated chemical compounds into the prime elements. If she gets an old-fashioned English teacher with horn-rimmed glasses, she'll have to diagram a lengthy, compound sentence into its component parts.

Education is really the process of crystallizing simple ideas from those with more complex structures. School is a prism that accepts the sunshine of general knowledge and splits it into a rainbow of individual hues we can actually see.

The idea persists that Christian education involves accumulating more data, adding more information to our storehouse of biblical knowledge. But Christian education also ought to be the process by which we burrow through our verbiage and doctrinal jargon to find the essence of our faith. Periodically we must reduce our Christianity to its least complicated form so we can be reminded just what it means to be Christian.

The Pharisees in Jesus' day were carrying excess baggage that needed to be discarded. They staggered under the load of laws, and interpretations of laws, and interpretations of interpretations. They needed to condense their faith, to wipe away the sludge of tradition that had buried God's desire. Unless we want to have their kind of ponderous spirituality, we must crystallize our faith from time to time and see it in its simplicity.

What does it mean to follow Jesus Christ? As straightforward as that question is, it has produced a mystifying variety of answers. Every inspirational book has a different reply to it; every radio preacher offers different counsel; every denomination seems to prescribe a different path. Like the people of the New Testament, we come with our desperate plea, "If thou be the Christ, tell us plainly," only to be rebuffed by confusion. The smorgasbord of spiritual solutions is so plentiful we can starve to death trying to make up our minds. Where shall we go for answers?

To Jesus, of course. We owe a great debt of gratitude to an unnamed lawyer who came to Christ three days before the Cross and asked him to crystallize the commandments. "'Teacher, which is the greatest commandment in the Law?' Jesus replied: 'Love the Lord your God with all your heart and with all your soul and with all your mind.' This is the first and greatest commandment. And the second is like it: 'Love your neighbor as yourself.' All the Law and the Prophets hang on these two commandments'" (Matt 22:36-40).

Reduce all of the law and prophets—all of those strange-sounding Levitical laws, all of those barbed, prophetic harangues, all of those Old Testament passages we avoid like castor oil—and they condense into love. You don't have to be a learned theologian with an impressive string of degrees to comprehend that. We are to love. Our charter, when all the doctrinal clutter is swept away, is to love God with our whole being and to love people as much as we love ourselves. That is what it means to keep the commandments.

The problem with that reduction is that it is not shocking enough. The subject of love has become trivial. Let someone sing, as Dionne Warwick did years ago, "What the World Needs Now Is Love, Sweet Love," and no one will disagree. Everybody is a cheerleader for love, but all of our enthusiastic rhetoric seldom leads to costly action.

Let the preacher thunder a message on love, and the congregation will yawn and give drowsy nods of agreement. Then the basses in the choir will slip into hidden slumber and the teenagers will go back to scribbling on the bulletin. Talk of love bores us. A preacher announcing that condensed Christianity is love is like a botanist calling a news conference to announce that grass is green. It is true, but hardly headline material.

But Jesus did say it, and if we're serious about knowing what it means to follow him, we should give credence to his words. The greatest commandment, he said, is loving God, and the second, inseparable one to it is loving people. The world will know you are mine, he said on another occasion, by the way you love.

Perhaps if we could take love off the crowded shelf of our minds and put it in the forefront where it could be examined and explored, Jesus' words would mean more to us. If we knew for certain that our calling is to love, and if we understood what love means, wouldn't we be motivated to keep the great commandment?

Before we try to look at love in a fresh way, notice how easily we sabotage Christianity by substituting other virtues for it. "And now these three remain: faith, hope and love. But the greatest of these is love" (1 Cor 13:13). Love is the supreme virtue and the golden residue that remains when the flame is put to real Christianity. Love is Christianity reduced to its smallest denominator. You would never guess it, however, if you would listen closely to our talk.

"The great commandment," we intone, "is being doctrinally sound. If you want to follow Jesus, you need to know the four spiritual laws, be able to define substitutionary atonement, and have the proper millennial view." We don't say it that bluntly, of course, but we imply it.

"The great commandment," we say, "is climbing the ladder of Christian piety. If you want to follow Jesus, you must worship, pray, witness, tithe, befriend the needy, and minister to your surly neighbor even though you can't stand her." We have a nifty checklist for separating the serious sheep from the backslidden goats.

"The great commandment," we say, "is building a successful church. We must enroll people, raise money, build buildings, preach sermons, and hire professional staff. The gates of hell cannot prevail against our efforts for God." We have equated the institutional church with the kingdom of God when the two are hardly synonymous.

Don't misunderstand and accuse me of taking potshots at some of our finest sacred cows. I believe we should be doctrinally literate, I am all for sincere piety, and I pastor an institutional church. If I am firing at those things, the target is pinned to my chest.

But I want you to see how easy it is to elevate those things above love. We can be doctrinally perfect, practice piety from sunrise to sunset, and grow a gigantic church—and never understand the indispensable kernel of Christianity. Unless we love God and love people, our deeds are as filthy rags. Though we have memorized the millennial chart, and though we have rubbed calluses on our knees in the prayer closet, and though we have built churches with impressive statistics, if we have not love, we are as sounding brass or a tinkling cymbal.

Most of us will never be lured from the faith by the glitter of the world or the teachings of a cult guru. We are too "Christian" to be enticed by obvious sin or every wind of new doctrine. We are not immune, though, from the subtle shift that makes genuine love secondary to propositional truth, piety, successful churchmanship, or some other noble tenet. We good Christians are not above being seduced by goodness.

But Jesus reminded us that love is the essential ingredient in our discipleship, so we must put it in its rightful place of top priority. How, then, do we love? How can we enliven love and make it attractive to us? Is it possible to see love with new eyes, to rediscover it as an old friend we just thought we knew? Can we fall in love with love again?

I am hesitant to try to answer those questions. Whatever I say will make me out to be an advice giver, an expert on love dispensing pearls of wisdom to those not so adept at loving. More than anyone, I know that posture is a charade. My lecturing you on love may be like a junior high coach lecturing Tom Landry on offensive football. Whatever I say on the subject of love can only be a primer for beginners. The sketches of love I draw are always stick figures.

But I will draw anyway in the hope that you will view love from a fresh angle. Trying to capture love in a few pages of a book is like trying to stuff a cloud in a suitcase, but I want to describe it the best I can. At the risk of sounding like a simplistic preacher reading from a sermon outline book, here are three things I believe about love.

First, I believe love is indispensable. Man is built to "run" on love. Just as an automobile runs on gasoline and lights run on electricity, so the human spirit "runs" on love. Love is the supreme virtue because human beings cannot live without it!

Every person in the world has an invisible "love tank." When that "love tank" is full, life goes well. When that "love tank" gets low, though, all kinds of problems rear their ugly heads. Some people sink into depression when they feel an absence of love. Some get angry or confused. Some get physically ill with headaches, ulcers, and even more serious ailments. Still others grow bitter and negative toward life. But though the symptoms vary from person to person, it is always true that an empty "love tank" leads to destruction.

William Hull, in his book *Love in Four Dimensions,* underscores the awful consequences of not being loved when he says, "While we need not minimize the threat of atomic annihilation, its destruction for many would be mercifully swift, whereas death from not being loved is always slow and painful. No bomb has been invented that can inflict as much cruelty on the vital core of our being as the blight of feeling that no one cares."[1]

The choice we human beings face can be expressed with stark simplicity: We love or we die.

As pastor of a suburban Baptist church, I see a steady trickle of people with needs. Some are physically sick, and some are emotionally sick. Some are grappling with marital problems, and some are battling the loneliness of life as a single adult. Some of the teenagers in our area are on drugs, and some of the young children in our neighborhood seem to have no respect at all for authority.

The one factor I would pinpoint as the ultimate source of pain in most of these people's lives is an absence of genuine love. It would be an oversimplification to say that all problems stem from a lack of love, but it would not be stretching the truth to say that a lack of love breeds most of the problems people have. It has been my observation that people who are loved deeply by family and friends have fewer physical and emotional problems than those who do not have that caring. All people have problems at times, and all people suffer. But those who know they are loved have fewer problems, and they are also better able to cope with the problems of life that do come their way.

The best gift we can give anyone is our love. We enhance a person's whole being when we care. Our husbands or wives need our love desperately. Our children cannot function without it. Our mothers and fathers need to have their "love tanks" filled on a regular basis. The people at the office and in the neighborhood—if they're normal, "happy" Americans—are starved for love.

It is high time we Christians understand the essence of our calling. We are called to be "love tank" fillers. We are the people who are in the business of healing others with the power of love.

A second thing I believe is that love is always personal. We do not love our church, our town, or our country; we can only love individual people. We can enjoy or appreciate groups, but love always has a singular focus. "I love old people" is a nonsense statement; "I love Mrs. Franklin wrapped in the patchwork quilt over there in the rocking chair" is a more accurate description of love. "I just love children," we are prone to exult. But unless we love hyperactive Johnny with the runny nose and missing front tooth, we don't have the faintest notion of the meaning of love.

Love particularizes. It hunts down specific people and showers them with attention. It knows names and the human idiosyncrasies that go with names. Love takes the time to know, to really know, its object. "Love in general" is a contradiction in terms.

Because love is personal, it demands more time from us than we are usually willing to give it. And most of us are too busy to love. If we are to love God with all our heart, we must spend time with him—time praying, dreaming, studying, worshiping. If we are to love another person, we must devote a good chunk of our life to that person. Who, in our frenzied age, has the time love requires?

What passes for love today, what we usually call love in our casual usages of the word, is not the love of the great commandment. We bounce off of God and people like the caroming ball in a pinball machine, thinking we are ringing up points for our loving deeds when, in reality, we have not loved at all. Our quick prayers, sporadic worship, hasty handshakes, boisterous slaps on the back, and casual conversation over the back fence do not qualify as "agape," self-giving love. Those deeds are fine, but let's not dupe ourselves into believing we're obeying the great commandment when we do them.

If we are to heed the great commandment about loving God and its corollary about loving people, we will have to narrow our focus. We will have to set our sights on God and a few people and say by our tangible caring, "You are important to me." I know we have been schooled since infancy to love everyone, but none of us can love everyone. At our best, we can love God and a handful of people. Be kind to the masses, yes. Smile at strangers in the supermarket, yes. But our love is always reserved for the few.

I have recently been made aware of this superficial, "pinball" approach in my own relationships. My life has become cluttered with trivial things that rob me of the time I need for love. I am acquainted with scores; of people, but my relationships tend to be the kind that, to use the Old Testament prophet's phrase, "heal the wounds of the people lightly." I stand guilty of the sin of attempting to "love in general" and am trying to move toward "love in particular."

I have given up loving the world. I will love my wife and two children and a few others, because I have neither the time nor the energy for more. But I will take comfort in the knowledge that loving God and a small group of people is closer to the great commandment than hurrying to reach the masses with a band-aid of momentary concern.

There is a third thing, too, that I think characterizes love, and it rides the coattail of this second one. Love acts. It moves beyond thoughts and feelings to action. I am in sympathy with all of those who tell us to verbalize our love, to tell people we love them. Saying "I love you" is admirable, and I should do it more. But I must admit I have a soft spot in my heart for those shy, nonverbal creatures who feel ill at ease spewing "I love you's" on everybody. If they live their "I love you's," that's message enough for me.

We have come to see love as warm and wordy. It is a spine-tingling feeling that issues forth syrupy verbiage. Love, we believe, feels and talks. Scripture, though, begs to differ. Love, the biblical writers said, *acts*. It always brings forth fruits. We validate our love with our feet and hands.

How can I honestly claim to love my son if I have no time to toss the baseball with him in the backyard? How can I sing that silly love song I've composed for my daughter if I have no time to attend her track meets? And should my wife believe my affections if I'm too busy to sip lemonade and dream with her as the sun sets?

My backyard baseball drills, trips to the track meets, and lawn chair conversations at sunset speak more eloquently about my love for my family than anything I could say. "Agape" love costs—in these cases I pay only a little time and energy and receive much pleasure in turn. But "agape" love can cost much more: sleepless hours by a hospital bed, painful sessions in the principal's office, thousands of dollars for life's necessities, fitful times of worry and frustration, long days of listening and weeping. Real love is willing to pay any price for another's benefit.

And when it comes to loving God the same is true. Our feet testify louder than our tongues. It is in our willingness to serve others, to worship faithfully, to give our money liberally, to live boldly in the face of our doubts, to seek his will and then follow it at all costs that we show our love for God. A love that talks may be a sham; a love that acts is inevitably genuine.

These three characteristics of love—its indispensability, its narrow focus, its verifiable action—are neither new nor revolutionary. If you have yawned your way through these last few pages, forgive me for lulling you with sameness. But if somehow we could hear afresh Christ's crystallizing summons to love, I think we would hear Good News. The great commandment is good news because it so clearly defines our calling. We are to love. Our first priority is not to debate theology, build impressive church buildings, make a lot of money, or astound the world with our piety. We are to love God and people with an indispensable, particular, active love.

The current religious scene is a maze of ideas and doctrines, enough to bewilder the most dedicated saint. Like laboratory rats poking for options, we are prone to get dizzy and lose our direction.

Then the lawyer comes with his question about the law and the prophets, and Jesus reduces all of it to love.

We have tasted of God's delicious grace, and we respond by loving him with our heart, soul, and mind, and loving others as ourselves. Then the walls in the maze tumble, and the one way becomes clear, and we know the direction we must go.

II.
THE DANCE HINDERED

In my house are many gods. With the boy, Jack Frost is ahead of Jesus, although we have never promoted Jack very hard. I see no harm in Jack and am not sure but what he ought to be taken into the church. He is a gifted spirit with an exciting technique and a rather gay program. And he is not terrible, like the Lord.

E. B. White in One Man's Meat

6.
Christian Caricatures

In the first five chapters, I have tried to lay a theological foundation for a faith that dances. I believe the five issues discussed in those chapters are necessary ingredients in a personal faith that will give us joy. If our commitment to Jesus is ever going to set our toes to tapping, we will:

(1) know our own story and admit our hunger for joy.
(2) understand that God is inviting us to dance.
(3) confess our humanity and give up the Sinless-and-Perfect Game.
(4) move from a transactional faith built on the law to a celebrational faith resting on grace.
(5) reduce our obligation to the twofold charge of the great commandment: love God and love others.

With that foundation laid, I want to turn in this section of the book to some hindrances to the dance. In the next four chapters, I will tackle some common obstacles that I think mute the gospel music and stifle our gladness.

In this chapter I single out a continual problem we will have to battle as we try to put more joy into our lives: Other Christians will unwittingly sap our enthusiasm. Even though we have those five linchpins firmly in place, the wheels of our theology can begin to wobble under the pressure of the current Christian scene. The kind of faith we're trying to build sets us at odds with many Christians, and their influence will tend to squelch our joy.

A careful pondering of my spiritual journey reveals one startling, ironic fact: Christians have done more to dissuade me from faith than non-Christians. Pornographers, drug pushers, secular humanists, and militant atheists have done little or nothing to douse my commitment to Christ. In fact, their presence in the world has probably nudged me into firmer conviction.

But I have attended scores of Christian meetings where my fervor took a nose-dive, watched dozens of Christian programs that pushed me toward agnosticism, and been in the presence of quite a few believers who diminished my joy. The saints have wreaked more havoc on my spiritual welfare than the sinners! Because of this realization, I now believe without question that one of the biggest deterrents to genuine faith is what I call "caricature Christianity."

A caricature is a likeness made laughable by one obviously overdrawn characteristic. The cartoonist's sketch of Jimmy Carter, for example, is definitely Jimmy Carter, but the sketch is funny because the ex-president's mouth is drawn out of proportion. Nixon's nose and Reagan's plastered hair are always enlarged and highlighted by the political cartoonists too, and the two presidents, for all their dignity, are rendered comical.

When I speak of "caricature Christianity," then, I am referring to a style of faith that is misshapen, and even grotesque, because one element is overdrawn. In surveying the demoralizing effect some Christians have had on me, I have been able to discern several distinct Christian caricatures. While I do not for a moment doubt the sincerity of those striking these postures, I have found it necessary, for my own faith's sake, to pinpoint what it is in each one that makes me squirm. Each caricature, I now see, is misshapen because it has been stretched and pulled by a particular facet of the American culture.

Here are the Christian caricatures I have observed, with a brief description of each.

The True Believer

The True Believer is infatuated with data. "Doubt" and "mystery" are not in the True Believer's dictionary. End-time charts, seminar notes, apologetics manuals, and chain-reference Bibles hold the key to finding the Sacred in life for these followers of Christ. For the True Believer, the Bible is a handy reference book that can be used to surmount any problem or answer any question. Those in this pose can be downright militant in their views and will never admit to uncertainty. "God said it, I believe it" is their answer when backed against a theological wall.

The tragic flaw in this caricature? It makes God a drab, celestial computer, and Christianity a boring memorization of the divine print-out.

The True Believer has been ensnared by the scientific and knowledge-oriented bent of modern culture.

The Zealous Witness

The Zealous Witness knows the "Roman road," carries tracts everywhere, and roams shopping malls looking for prospects. Chances are, he or she has attended an evangelistic training class and knows the latest techniques: Ask about hobbies and interests, show genuine concern, and then pop the spiritual questions. The Zealous Witness is long on boldness and woefully short on sensitivity. Those in this pose make Jesus sound as attractive as the latest labor-saving gadget and as necessary as the cemetery plot at Rolling Hills.

For all of its courageous sincerity, this caricature makes sharing the Good News of Christ first cousins with selling vacuum cleaners. The Zealous Witness has been seduced by the marketing methods of capitalism.

The Successful Optimist

The Successful Optimist will always have a grin, a handshake, and a positive thought for you. Those Christians in this pose have hand-stitched mottoes hanging in their living rooms and offices: "Nothing Is Impossible," "If You Think You Can, You Can," "God Wants You to Win." Winning is, in fact, one of their main themes, and winning is measured in terms of "stuff": cars, clothes, stock, and other material things. The Successful Optimist sees God as the Heavenly Slot Machine just waiting to dole out blessings to those who know how to pull the handle.

But Successful Optimist doesn't know how to lose, and it never has really scrutinized the persecuted peasant from Nazareth. It has been captured by the climb-the-ladder-of-success mentality of big business.

The Misty-Eyed Mystic

The Misty-Eyed Mystic is adrift in a sea of emotion. Worship, for those in this camp, is an exercise in trying to conjure chills and goose bumps. This style of Christianity puts out fleeces, talks incessantly of the Spirit, and prays regularly for rescue out of difficult situations. It has a great interest in the Shroud of Turin, the healings at Lourdes, the millennium, and the time Uncle Billy heard Jesus tell him to buy the stock that eventually made him a millionaire.

But the Misty-Eyed Mystic is also a product of the contemporary scene: He or she is a card-carrying member of the ever-popular If-It-Feels-Good-Do-It Society. The Mystic actually worships at a common secular shrine: Self-Gratification.

The Efficient Professional

One would assume that the refuge from impersonal technology, subtle manipulation, and slick programming would be the church. Surely the community that follows the loving Christ would be a haven from such demonic things. But even a quick glance at the current ecclesiastical picture reveals otherwise.

The most "successful" churches are run like the most successful big corporations. So it comes as no surprise that the Efficient Professional is widely heralded in the ecclesiastical world. Men and women who are unemotional, skilled administrators are highly sought for pastoral positions and committee assignments. They see themselves as "facilitators" and believe the church could best improve itself by purchasing a computer to mass-produce "letters of concern" to absentees.

Somehow the Efficient Professional seems far, far removed from the one who roamed the dusty roads of Galilee without even a place to lay his head. The Efficient Professional is but the religious version of cybernetic society's hero: the cold and competent one who gets things done.

The Liberated Activist

The five previously mentioned caricatures describe Christians who usually appear on the conservative end of the theological spectrum (though the Efficient Professional is no doubt admired in liberal circles too). The conservative, evangelical wing of the faith is where I spend most of my time, and thus I've had more opportunity to observe people there. But lest we forget those to the theological left, these last two caricatures describe aberrations of the liberal wing.

The Liberated Activist has a passion for social issues and a disdain for fundamentalists. Often this person is in reaction to a rigid style of religion taught and practiced by his or her parents. So, the Liberated Activist not only champions social causes but feels compelled to parade a "freed up" version of the faith to others. Once taboo practices, such as smoking, drinking, and cursing, are worn openly as badges of freedom.

The Liberated Activist finds traditional prayer a waste of time and, instead, follows the revolutionary Christ who overturned the money-changers' tables. The emphasis here is on action and change.

But these freed up activists, ironically, are as judgmental as the fundamentalists, and for all their freedom, they are in bondage to nonconformity. They have fallen victim to the paranoid slogan that says "whatever is 'in' is 'out' for us."

The Eclectic Intellectual

The Eclectic Intellectual sees modern evangelicalism as naive, uninformed, and dogmatic. To appear judgmental of others, though, is the unpardonable sin. For the Eclectic Intellectual, Christianity is the sum of all the loving deeds and ideas in history. Gandhi, in reality, was as Christian as the apostle Paul because he was a man of love and justice. His creed is insignificant.

But these tolerant ones have a fatal flaw too: They make the Christian Way flimsy by removing its doctrinal backbone. In trying to be open-minded, they so water down Christianity that it becomes bland and tasteless. The Eclectic Intellectuals have been seduced by the "miscellaneous mentality" of the age that gathers ragbag scraps from assorted places and tries to make a seamless robe of them.

Now that I have sketched these seven caricatures, let me make four summary comments about them.

First, each caricature embodies a significant truth. The problem with these distortions is not that they're untrue, but that they're *too true*. Who can deny the validity of each caricature's overriding virtue: the Believer's conviction, the Witness's boldness, the Optimist's happiness, the Mystic's emotion, the Professional's competence, the Activist's social conscience, the Intellectual's open-mindedness? Those are wonderful qualities, but heresy is nothing more than truth blown out of proportion, and these caricatures are heretical precisely because they magnify one facet of Christian truth to the exclusion of other Christian truths. Remember, the cartoonist's picture of Jimmy Carter was comical not because the grin was wrong but because it was *too right*. A caricature is laughable because one characteristic is exaggerated to such an extent that it overshadows others.

Second, several of these caricatures can be found simultaneously in one person. Sadly, faith deformities often come in bunches. Like the poor fellow with big ears, bug eyes, and a bulbous, red nose, some saints are afflicted with more than one misshapen feature. When this happens, the results are grotesque and even tragic. The joyous way of Christ becomes unrecognizable, and the Christian Way appears to be a cheap carnival of sideshow attractions. I think most people who resist Christianity are not resisting Christianity at all. They are resisting a deformed version of it that would be unappealing to any thinking person.

Third, it is possible to move from one caricature to another. I think, at some point in my life, I have assumed each of the seven poses I've mentioned. The reason I can write about them is that I've lived them. If this chapter smacks of name-calling and pigeonholing, my defense is that I am the accused as well as the accuser. I have played the role of spiritual chameleon well. I know full well that today's True Believer may be tomorrow's Eclectic Intellectual. The Liberated Activist may, through a series of life events, one day become the Successful Optimist. The spiritual life is a life of continual movement, and I think most growing Christians move in and out of these caricatures as they develop spiritually.

Fourth, we do not have to be overly dismayed by these caricatures. After all, the church is full of sinners, and forgiveness is the touchstone of the gospel. The vital thing for each of us is not to cast stones at others we see as misguided or to decide that Christianity is a farce because it produces so many weird people. No, the vital thing for us is to renew our private pledges to build a faith that is solid, credible, and passionate. Caricature Christianity has frequently sent me into depression and anger, but I have gradually learned that distorted believers do not have to set the sail for *my* journey with God. I am captain of my own spiritual ship. How others navigate theirs is between them and God. I do not have to criticize, become cynical, or feel haughty that I'm so spiritually mature. I just have to be true to the Spirit who is rummaging around in *my* soul.

Our response to the Christian caricatures around and within us is important. Should we adopt a middle-of-the-road, Laodicean faith that avoids the extremes of the caricatures? Should we downplay our beliefs, our witness, our emotions, our optimism, etc., for fear of being grotesque? Am I suggesting that we never "get carried away"?

No, no, and no. But I do think we should be aware of these caricatures, for any time our faith becomes distorted, the cause of Christ suffers. And sickness, throughout history, has often disguised itself as spirituality. An occasional spiritual checkup has to be good for us.

Jesus, as always, is our best guide and model. Even the brief sketches of his life we have in the Gospels show us this: He is too mysterious for the True Believers, too subdued for the Zealous Witnesses, too much a failure for the Successful Optimists, too sensible for the Misty-Eyed Mystics, too personal for the Efficient Professionals, too pious for the Liberated Activists, and too stringent for the Eclectic Intellectuals.

May we be the same.

7.

The Thomas Syndrome

The apostle Thomas has gotten a lot of bad press through the years. His name has become synonymous with doubt, and those not schooled in Scripture may actually think Thomas is his last name: Doubting Thomas. Most of the sermons preached about Thomas chide him for his unbelief and exhort the listener to shun doubt and cling to an unwavering faith.

I am not sure we have treated Thomas fairly, though, and for years I've had the inclination to defend him. My taking up for Thomas is a sort of self-defense, I think, because I identify strongly with his quest for truth. In taking up for Thomas, I am also taking up for myself and my insistence that commitment be built on a solid foundation. Though separated by two thousand years of history, Thomas and I share the desire to have verifiable data for our faith.

When I was a seminary student, I sat one evening in our recliner in the cracker-box, frame house where we lived and waited for God to reveal himself. It was a confusing time for me, doubts were creeping into my mind, and some pivotal questions stared me in the face.

"God, if you are real," I prayed, "give me a sign of your presence. I will wait right here in this recliner until you make yourself known. Give me a Damascus Road experience, and I will never doubt you again. Show me plainly your will for my life."

I waited long into the night for God to come, for a voice to sound, even for the phone to ring. I would have gladly settled for a still, small voice. What I got was stone cold silence.

That was my own version of John 20:25, I suppose: "Unless I see the nail marks in his hands and put my finger where the nails were, and put my hand into his side, I will not believe." Like Thomas I wanted proof. Unlike Thomas the revelation I requested never came. At least he got to touch the risen Christ; I touched only darkness and found it frustrating. Some speak brazenly of knowing the will of God. For me, groping for God's will felt—and still feels—frighteningly similar to flying by the seat of my own breeches.

But still I believed. A spark of faith could not be extinguished even by that cold silence, and in dozens of ways since then the spark has been kept aglow. God has never been as audible and visible as I wish, and, with Paul, I look at life every day "through a glass darkly." But if pressed to give the reason for my existence, I always come back to the God who speaks to me in silence and touches me with invisible hands. I am one of those who has not seen and yet, in a faltering, complaining way, has believed.

Thomas, then, is my brother, and in defending him I am defending *us*. I think he is not so much to be condemned for his doubt as commended for his thoughtful commitment. He was not flippant about his relationship to God, nor would he be swayed by emotion. He wanted evidence and legitimate experience, and for that he is to be applauded. None of this cheap, "sweet" faith for him.

Every church needs a Thomas. He is the one who stands in the midst of the heated business meeting and recites the needed facts to quiet the fray. He is the one who says, "Let's think this over. Let's get all the facts. Let's not rush into anything." Calm and calculating, Thomas had the knack for getting down to the significant. He was practical and not about to climb out on a whimsical limb.

You have to wonder how Thomas and Peter managed to coexist in the same band of disciples. If ever two men seem to clash in temperament and style, it is these two. Thomas was the careful assembler and discerner of data, compiling evidence before venturing into decisions. Peter was the rambunctious, devil-may-care sort who jumped first and thought about it later. Perhaps Christ knew his band needed both: Thomas for calculation, Peter for motivation. Maybe he knew the disciples needed Thomas for practicality and Peter for passion.

In looking at the scant biblical material we have on Thomas, I have concluded that his most serious flaw was not doubt. His doubt was actually a stepping stone to deeper trust. I believe Thomas's biggest problem was this: He was so careful and thorough he nearly missed the Resurrection. If we can fault him at all, it is because he was so "geared in" to knowledge, understanding, and evidence that he wasn't open to astonishment. In looking for facts, in other words, Thomas was nearly blind to miracles.

In addition to his famous refusal to believe the Resurrection, Thomas also probed for facts on a previous occasion. In the midst of Jesus' poetic promise about eternity in John 14, Thomas interrupted to ask, "Lord, we don't know where you are going, so how can we know the way?" Thomas could not be content with generalities; he wanted details. He yearned to know where and how this promise about "many rooms and mansions" would be fulfilled.

I think Thomas was the kind of person who had a hard time with the Resurrection even *after* he was confronted with indisputable evidence. The Cross and Resurrection just wouldn't "compute" in his mind. He was probably like the friar in the Nebraska monastery living "sanely and sensibly, hour after hour, day after day." He was the accountant, punching his calculator to make sure the figures add up, or the scientist, observing his test tube for proof of a theorem. Talk of resurrection was for religious fanatics and ignorant dreamers. Thomas was too smart to be hoodwinked by the hallucination of the depressed disciples.

Why was he so precise and calculating? How did he come by his cautious ways? Perhaps it was just stamped into his personality. Don't you know someone who prices pot roasts at four different supermarkets before buying one? Don't you have at least one friend who would rather stay in a secure job with little intrigue than gamble with a new one? Some people are just cut out of that bolt of cloth. Their personality breeds caution and perfectionism.

Or perhaps Thomas came from a family of "data discerners." He may have grown up in an emotionless, intelligent family that placed a premium on knowledge. His careful mindset may have been handed him by equally precise family members.

Or he could have been reacting to something in his society that triggered his calculating approach to life. Perhaps Thomas saw in the mystery religions of his day—with their burning of incense and "mood" music and stress on emotions—something to be avoided at all costs. Perhaps the grandiose messianic hopes of his fellow Jews caused him to react with caution and not get "carried away." Perhaps the dreams of the disciples for power and glory "turned him off" and pushed him to try to find a genuine faith built on solid evidence.

But for whatever reason, Thomas was a "fact man," a seeker of knowledge, a pilgrim in search of the city called "Truth." And before we hastily reach for stones to throw in his direction, let's at least recognize again the strength in Thomas's way of doing things. After all, religion can be abused. None of us wants to build a life on a fairy tale void of historical fact. Our faith needs a good dose of Thomas's approach, or we'll find ourselves mired in an ignorance that we can only try to cover up with tambourines and raucous "Jesus songs." We can learn a good lesson from Thomas.

But we can also learn from his mistake. I call Thomas's careful, never-commit-yourself-until-you-have-all-the-evidence approach to life the "Thomas Syndrome," and I see signs of it all around. The Thomas Syndrome is in effect whenever we react to some error of emotional excess by pulling back too far in the other direction, whenever we equate the Christian life only with doctrinal correctness and dry, orthodox sermons. Any time we are so fearful of getting out on an emotional limb that we fail to climb the tree, the Thomas Syndrome has us in its joy-killing grasp.

And this careful, no-risk approach to life does just that—it chokes our joy. Any Christian afflicted with the Thomas Syndrome is destined to march through life with antiseptic caution, never making mistakes or taking chances. The Thomas Syndrome makes one "the morally consti-pated, dyspeptic, up-tight, good person who has never gone to the party or held a red balloon in his hot little fist."[1] When Thomas becomes our role model—and he is the patron saint of the church in this scientific, logical age—dancing is unthinkable. Meticulous marching to doctrinal commands becomes the order of the day, and joy takes a nose-dive.

Are you a victim of the Thomas Syndrome? Here are ten questions that can help you answer that question:

(1) Do you believe that miracles still happen?
(2) Have you taken a big risk—remarried, changed jobs, written a book, tried out for the PGA golf tour, gone back to school—within the past year?
(3) Have you taken a small risk—changed your hairstyle, tried a new food, introduced yourself to a neighbor, taken tennis lessons, entered a "fun run"—within the past month?
(4) Have you done something "just for fun" this week (taken the family for an ice cream cone, gone to a movie, bought a record album, read a good book)?
(5) Would you welcome some innovative experiment in your church's worship?
(6) Have you laughed until you cried in the last three months?
(7) Have you recently changed your mind about some social or theo-logical issue?
(8) Do you pray and read the Bible with expectancy?

(9) Can you talk about your faith without being defensive when someone differs with you?

(10) Do you have a dream that puts sparkle in your days?

If you answered "no" to three or more of those questions, you have possibly been snared by the Thomas Syndrome. Your desire for security and knowledge has robbed you of your joy. Like Thomas you have assembled the data and have the pertinent facts implanted in your head, but the miracle of living and the astonishing implications of the Resurrection have escaped you. You are conservative, orthodox—and sorely lacking in adventure!

The interesting thing about this seductive siphoning of our joy—and those of us who have succumbed to it can take some comfort in this—is that the Thomas Syndrome usually strikes perceptive, faithful people. It is a malady reserved for those wise enough to see the abuse and misuse of Christianity and serious enough to want a credible commitment. The Thomas Syndrome does not affect the superficially religious or those wanting an emotional "high." It does its dastardly work on the intelligent saints who want to flee spiritual sham and know the truth.

Thomas's followers are astute enough to spot the flaws in the fabric of modern spirituality. They know all about the caricatures I described in the last chapter. They know that what passes for a miracle in someone's life is usually wishful thinking, that prayer all too often degenerates into bargaining with God for personal "goodies," that evangelism is frequently a game played by "gospel hawkers," that the church often stumbles into a bureaucratic institutionalism that neglects little people. And in seeing these glaring abuses, Thomas's people refuse to "buy into" miracle, prayer, evangelism, and church. They will not applaud these things just because others want them to. They demand to see the wounds before believing the Resurrection.

So, it is these perceptive truth-seekers who feel the deadening effects of the Thomas Syndrome. Their admirable quest for proof leads them into the alley of monotonous caution. Looking only for reasoned integrity, they find meticulous boredom. The abundant life of which Jesus spoke eventually becomes the impossible dream.

What do we do when we realize we are too cautious, too sensible, too cynical? How do we escape the Thomas Syndrome? I offer you a concise plan for alleviating the numbing pain of this prevalent evangelical ailment.

First, we can admit our condition. Like our brothers and sisters in Alcoholics Anonymous, we can begin our recovery by confessing that we have a problem. As a longtime sufferer of the Thomas Syndrome, I found great personal relief in confessing my uptight cynicism. I am gifted with the dubious ability to find something to sneer at in every modern expression of Christianity. I can attend any church in my city and come home depressed. It was a painful but helpful day, then, when I realized my own haughtiness. Those churches might have a problem, but so do I. I am too analytical and judgmental, too deeply entrenched in my own spiritual rut to grant freedom to those in different ruts, too sensible most days to kick up my heels and dance. Admitting we are drab disciples is not easy, but necessary.

Second, we can walk our own way. As I mentioned in the last chapter, we do not have to be swayed by someone else's spirituality. Why can't we be secure in walking the way we sense God is leading us? Why do we feel sub-Christian (or super-Christian) when we are in the presence of believers of a different stripe? Our defensiveness reveals our lack of faith in what God is doing in our lives. Certainly it puzzles us that the same Spirit can lead people in such divergent directions, but we cannot answer for others. We must walk our way, step to our drummer, and dance to the music we hear. When we can gladly grant other believers the freedom to do the same, we'll know we've been cured of our disease.

Third, we can loosen up. Like Thomas, most of us are too tight and programmed. We think being Christian means becoming serious adults when, in reality, it means becoming playful children. We can measure our spiritual condition, I think, more by our laughter than our labor.

To counteract the Thomas Syndrome, we will have to consciously choose to relax, count more stars, read more stories, follow our foolish hearts to hilarity. Our Jesus is too one-sided—too somber, too stern, and too concerned only about correctness. We need the Jesus who swapped yarns and went to parties. We need the Jesus who can teach us how to look life in the eye and laugh at it.

Let's be candid enough to admit the seriousness of our disease. The Thomas Syndrome is nearly impossible to cure. At best, we might be able to keep it from being fatal.

Any twentieth century adult, incubated in a scientific culture and nurtured in a legalistic church, will have a hard time shaking the Thomas Syndrome. Our age naturally produces careful, sensible people. The man or woman who will confess the folly of the Thomas Syndrome, try to walk a solitary road, and make strides in loosening up to receive life's gifts will be the exception, not the rule. My brother Thomas will continue to lure most people into his fact-finding fold.

But if we ever hope to dance in our relationship to Christ, we will finally have to part ways with Thomas. We will have to take from him some crucial qualities of faith—his honesty, his passion for understanding, his love of apologetics—but then leave him as he solemnly flips through his concordance.

He will hunt for data while we probe for miracles. He will browse the library while we tell jokes at the domino parlor. He will march to the words of the Gospel while we spend our day dancing to its tune.

8.
Redefining Christian Witness

Best to come clean and admit the truth up front: I have always been intimidated by evangelism. The occasion of the "witnessing button" that I described earlier is but one of many terrifying experiences I have had in trying to bear witness for Christ. Since boyhood I have been told to share my faith with others. Indeed, I have been told that any serious Christian could scarcely keep from spilling the Good News on others, that the Living Water within me would just naturally overflow onto the parched lives around me."For the real believer, "my mentors said, "telling people about Jesus is as natural as breathing."

For better or worse, that has not been my experience. I have knocked on doors, quoted Scripture verses, and related my personal testimony with feigned confidence. I have preached revivals, attended evangelism conferences, and supposedly learned the skills necessary to be an effective Christian persuader. I have even loudly proclaimed to others the necessity of boldly proclaiming the faith. But in all honesty, I have done most of my evangelizing with a sense of dread. Personal witnessing has been one of those necessary Christian duties that has made me feel guilty and "unspiritual." How can I declare myself a serious follower of Jesus Christ, I've wondered, when I don't even have the nerve to tell my beer-drinking neighbor about him?

Because witnessing has been such a heavy obligation for me, it has been one of those biblical mandates that has kept me from dancing. All of those biblical admonitions to "tell the world" have sounded to me like marching orders from a drill sergeant. And, from the samplings I've taken from the general evangelical community, I'm not alone in my discomfort. Many "serious Christians" seem to share my distaste for evangelism. Many join me in wondering how an order to blab the mystery of our deepest treasure can ever sound like good news.

I envy those who can talk of the Cross in casual conversation, who can speak of Jesus as calmly as they speak of the latest heat spell or the score of last night's ball game. I wish I could evangelize without sweaty palms, but I can't. My journey with Christ is so sacred and private any attempt to articulate it freezes in my throat.

But I am also a bit suspicious of anyone too glib about sacred things. I am not comfortable when someone tells me of his latest sexual rendezvous, for instance, because sex to me is a sacred experience not to be paraded before the world. Nor do I want to hear someone tell me of his last conversation with a dying parent, or his touching dialogue with a baby daughter at bedtime, or his wife's struggle with menopause. Those are private things, not to be shouted to casual acquaintances. When someone glibly tells me of such things I feel party to trampling on the sacred. If we speak of the deep things of life without a tremor in our voice, we have forgotten how to love.

So when the preacher implores me to buttonhole strangers in the shopping mall and tell them my testimony, I rebel. I will not cast my spiritual pearls before busy people on the way to the afternoon movie. Don't ask me to relate the most precious experiences of my life to disinterested strangers. If I tell my testimony at all, I will do it when the time is right, when someone has "ears to hear" it.

You see my dilemma. Probably you face it too. How do we obey the biblical command to "tell the world" and keep our integrity intact? How can we evangelize without cheapening our gospel? How can we witness for Christ in a way that is both effective and genuine?

All of us must decide for ourselves how to answer those questions. Our personality, experiences, and life situation will determine how we should best bear our Christian witness. No one can write an evangelism book that will apply to everyone. An evangelist admonishing all Christians to witness for Christ the same way is as ridiculous as a shoe salesman recommending the same shoe size for all feet. If the shoe fits, wear it, but by all means don't feel obligated to make someone else's stereotypical approach to evangelism your own.

As for me, the "old evangelism" taught me by my mentors just didn't fit. I kept trying to squeeze into it, but it was a joy-killing strain. Through it all, though, I have learned that if I am to "tell the world" on the one hand, and sustain my joy on the other, I will have to have a "new evangelism," an evangelism not made of tracts, door knocking, and week-long revivals. That shoe may have fit my mentors, but my feet are too hesitant and timid to wear it.

Somewhere in my head, my philosophy of Christian influence lies tangled like a ball of fishing line in a tackle box. I want to unravel it here. As I try to redefine Christian witness and make it less a guilt—including obligation, I find several key ideas are crucial.

The "new evangelism" will be new. Modern evangelism has for years borrowed its methodology from one primary source: big business. We have learned to relate our faith the way a salesman sells his product, and the results of this approach have been more sad than comical—sad because we have commercialized Jesus and packaged him as a necessary appendage to "the good life." As Virginia Stem Owens puts it, "Where the spirit needs nourishing by dreams and visions, we are substituting the junk food of media hype, convinced that if such tactics can sell detergent they can also sell Jesus."[1]

Selling Jesus is a losing proposition. Try as we might to put him in an expensive, three-piece suit with matching silk tie, he persists in wearing a robe and tattered sandals. How can that image ever catch the eye of a society hooked on "flash"? And while we would like to hold him up as a member of the million dollar round table, he goes right on about the business of touching the infirm and hanging out with losers. How are we going to sell that to people climbing the ladder of success? And the Cross? How in the world can we ever dress up the Cross enough to make it enticing to a generation living by the pleasure principle?

No, Jesus is not a good product, but we have taken the big business techniques of confrontation, manipulation, and image advertising and tried our best. Even those who give assent to our persuasion scarcely know that their Lord is not a possibility thinker with a toothy smile but a celibate vagrant with no clout and a cross on his back.

If we are going to do true evangelism, evangelism that truthfully and accurately holds up Jesus, big business will not do for our model. Big business by its very nature feels the pulse of society and accommodates itself to it. Jesus, on the other hand, invites society to feel his pulse and accommodate itself to him. He is resolute in his desire not to be packaged and sold as a popular product.

However we choose to spread the Good News of God's love in Christ, we will have to do it in a way that doesn't cheapen that news with "techniques." We need an evangelism that is new in method and style—even if it doesn't sell.

The "new evangelism" will be indirect. Not totally perhaps, but the persuasion that will best convey the gospel in the main will be subtle and indirect. The "hard sell" is no good when telling our deepest secrets.

Sören Kierkegaard, the nineteenth-century Danish philosopher and theologian, wrestled with the confident apathy of his countrymen and advocated an indirect approach in telling them of Christ. Anyone who has been brutalized by a verbal evangelistic onslaught knows the validity of Kierkegaard's analogy: "In sawing wood it is important not to press down too hard on the saw; the lighter the pressure exerted by the sawyer, the better the saw operates. If a man were to press down with all his strength, he would no longer be able to saw at all."[2]

In recent times, Fred Craddock, relying heavily on Kierkegaard's writings, has suggested the indirect approach for our day too. In his book *Overhearing the Gospel*, Craddock encourages the gospel teller to use the indirect method of the storyteller:

> A good storyteller seldom looks at anyone. Some whittle, some look into the glowing fireplace, some never stop walking down the lane, and others lie on the hillside looking at the stars while chewing tender stems of wild grass. They save their eye contact for those occasional didactic turns, when there is a lesson to be planted on the forehead. But stories are always overheard and in that overhearing there may well be encounter and confrontation. These are experiences of the listener, not tactics of a speaker who does not realize that some moments are allowed to happen, not made to happen.[3]

This indirect approach to communication clashes with popular evangelistic methods. We know only of confrontation and frontal assault, of saying our piece and then brashly refuting the listener's excuses. That direct, aggressive approach will surely persuade some people, and there will always be a place for it. But there is no telling how many people will always be deaf to an evangelistic approach that smacks of hard-hitting salesmanship.

The "new evangelism" will know how to "fish for men." The vogue now is to go fishing with a club, chase the fish around the pond, and then conk them on the head. That method does yield a catch, and many will testify to its effectiveness. But we need to learn how to fish with tantalizing lures that prick interest and stimulate curiosity. When people discover the gospel *on their own* and taste its life-renewing flavor, they will be "hooked" for good.

This indirect style of communication obviously will have implications for our preaching and teaching. It will move us away from the method of laying out our logical points and drawing conclusions for the listener to a style of telling stories and dropping hints. But indirect evangelism will also affect our conversations, our everyday give-and-take. We will look for opportunities to speak a needed word, to plant a seed, to pass along a book, to invite a friend to church. We will not be pressured to hammer the message of Christ into others but will instead drop it gently all around them and then pray that it will take root and grow.

The "new evangelism" will see time as a friend. "Urgency" has long been one of the bywords of evangelism. I have been urged many times to "tell the world" as quickly as possible because time is running out. Certainly there is truth in that encouragement. Certainly the Christian has news too good to keep. But that "hurry up" approach to persuasion discourages intimacy and tends to make the witness a hawker peddling his wares for quick gain.

The "new evangelism" will see time not as an enemy stalking people but as an ally calling us into deeper relationships. It will see time on our side, working with us to break down the barriers that separate us from others. When time is seen as a friend, we know that we can sip coffee with a neighbor, fish with a coworker, play bridge with the club—and do it all as relaxed evangelism. We don't have to rush, to push our relationships, to outrun the Holy Spirit. Because time is a friend, we can be ourselves and trust God to use us in the context of normal existence.

When evangelism is too urgent it makes for red-faced, straining relationships. But when time is seen as our ally, we can be relaxed, genuine people who know that God uses us naturally. The pressure to cajole and coerce vanishes, and evangelism becomes not a frenzied program but a loving way of life.

The "new evangelism" will not be afraid of silence. One word I have tried to avoid in this book is "share." I have not avoided it completely, but I have used it sparingly because the word is so overworked in Christian circles. The word "share" is a good one, and the concept it symbolizes is certainly biblical. But we've "shared" testimonies, "shared" money, "shared" fellowship, "shared" truth, and "shared" other things so much I'm about "shared" out.

This prevalence of "sharing" is symptomatic of our wordiness. "Sharing our witness" to most of us means saying things—reciting Scripture, telling our testimony, speaking sermons. But the "new evangelism" will recognize that effective persuasion also involves silence, a silence that novelist Walker

Percy suggests is itself an invitation: "In these times everyone is an apostle of sorts, ringing doorbells and bidding his neighbor to believe this and do that. In such times, when everyone is saying 'Come!' when radio and television say nothing but 'Come!' it may be that the best way to say 'Come' is to remain silent. Sometimes silence itself is a 'Come!'"[4]

Silence actually contributes three things to our impact on the world.

First, it guards our own inner fire. In *The Way of the Heart*, Henri Nouwen reminds us of this benefit of silence:

> What needs to be guarded is the life of the Spirit within us. Especially we who want to witness to the presence of God's Spirit in the world need to tend the fire within with utmost care. It is not so strange that many ministers have become burnt-out cases, people who say many words and share many experiences, but in whom the fire of God's Spirit has died and from whom not much more comes forth than their own boring, petty ideas and feelings. Sometimes it seems that our many words are more an expression of our doubt than our faith. It is as if we are not sure that God's Spirit can touch the hearts of people: we have to help him out and, with many words, convince others of his power. But it is precisely this wordy unbelief that quenches the fire.[5]

Nouwen also quotes an early church father who likened continual speaking to leaving the door of a steam bath open. When the door is always open the heat escapes, he said. And when the door of speech is always open we lose our fire. Only silence can tend the inner fire and keep it glowing.

Second, silence allows us to listen. So much of our evangelism strikes me as a haughty, one-way conversation with a deaf world. We assume the posture of clever answer-men trying to pound our theological propositions into hard hearts. Silence enables us to listen, to hear each person clearly, to respect each person's story. Our silence speaks more forcefully of our love than our preaching. After all, communication is a matter of words, but communion takes place only in silence.

Third, silence gives us opportunity to act. "I'd rather see a sermon than hear one any day," the old poem says, and while the idea has become trite, it still carries a significant truth. Words are cheap. Though we speak with the tongues of men and of angels, if we do not have love—if we do not sacrifice, if we do not laugh, if we do not listen, if we have no life within us—our words have the empty clang of a loud cymbal. I don't believe the world is much impressed with our eloquence; it wants to see personal love in action. And in the silence we can shut up and get busy.

The "new evangelism" will respect the sovereignty of God. "You might be the only Bible some people will ever read," my mentors told me. If so, let me be the first to say that "someone" is in trouble. If that person's relationship to God depends totally on my goodness and my influence, that person is doomed. And if I have to live with the pressure of being a living Bible, I will buckle under the strain. I am, quite frankly, a poor model of God and am forced to cling to his forgiving grace like a drowning man clutching a life preserver.

Whatever those biblical passages about predestination and election mean, they are a needed reminder to us nervous witnesses that God "has it all together." As unbelievable as it seems, he can do fine without me. Surely I am accountable for my actions, and certainly I must try to nudge others toward him, but ultimately God is in control. He is sovereign. He calls his own sheep and knows each one by name.

John Baillie writes, "Few things are so important in the spiritual life as to be able to distinguish God's burden from our own."[6] That seems to me to be a needed word when it comes to evangelism. Though some would make us feel guilty about our burden for "soul winning," the truth is that "soul winning" is God's business. God has assumed the burden of calling people to himself, and every person must privately respond to that divine tug at the heart. Our part is to respond to our personal tug and to live our faith with integrity. Whenever we assume God's burden of salvation we set ourselves up for misery.

Thank God, he is sovereign! We do not have to worry and fret and force him on others. His Spirit is quite capable of getting the job done. We can relax and celebrate our own relationship with him. And we can know that if that relationship is real, it will be evident and will itself become one of God's tools of reconciliation.

Last week a young woman visited me in my office at the church. During our conversation she began to tell me about her husband, a man I have never met who has never attended our church. He came from a strict religious home, she said, and as a boy was at church every time the doors opened. But as an adult he became disenchanted with what he saw as the manipulative, pressured style of his church back home. He decided he didn't need that in his life and vowed not to frequent church anymore. Now his family comes to our church every Sunday, and he sits at home, resentful and disillusioned.

That story, or a similar version of it, is one I have heard frequently. We have statistics on the number of people who respond to our evangelistic campaigns and confess Christ publicly. There is no accurate way of telling, however, how many people have sworn off Christ and his church because of an aggressive, sales-oriented approach to evangelism. Those people, like the disgruntled husband I've just described, quietly shuffle off into oblivion and never make anybody's head-count. But the story of many silent, offended protesters can be heard if we listen closely enough.

My point is not that traditional evangelism is evil but that it is inadequate for many modern listeners. My conversation with the woman last week revealed her husband to be a shy, sensitive loner who loves his family and leads a moral life. His wife believes him to be a Christian, and I pray she is right. But he will never be reached by contemporary methods of outreach. Confrontational questions about his spiritual condition will only send him scurrying into further retreat. Only someone who will respect his privacy, get to know him personally, and offer Christ indirectly will have a chance of moving that man toward God's kingdom. The "new evangelism" I have tried to outline in this chapter is the only hope for reaching him.

Some people will simply never be reached by the "old evangelism." And many committed, sincere Christians will never see themselves as witnesses at all if that is the only model they have. If evangelism is aggressive confrontation, the sanguine and choleric temperaments among us might do well. But what about the phlegmatic and melancholic Christians who by nature are repulsed by aggressiveness and "put off" by salesmanship? Should we just exclude them from witnessing because their temperaments aren't right? Should we tell the frail marathoners in our midst that they have to put on the pads and play linebacker or we have no place for them on the team?

In redefining Christian witness, I am trying to broaden the scope of evangelism. I want the marathoner to find his sport and run with all of his heart. I want the sensitive loner who is deaf to evangelistic "push and shove" to meet a Christian who understands him. I want followers of Jesus Christ to quit speaking "churchese" and just be real people. I want all of us to know that Christian witnessing is not pushing propositions but living a life of radical love. And I want all of those pressured evangelists marching to Zion to ease up and dance a little bit—for only when the world sees them dancing will it want what they have to offer.

9

When the Music Stops

Not long ago I caught a young driver doing what I often do—singing along with the car radio. I watched him for a good while and got tickled at his gyrations. Not only was he singing, he was tapping, swaying, and nodding as well. At a traffic light, he glanced over at me, mid-contortion, and realized what a strange sight he was. He smiled sheepishly and became as still as a stone. I was immediately sorry for staring and wished I hadn't stifled his ecstasy.

Had I been listening to the rhythm of that tune on the radio, I might have been gyrating too. My family used to scold me for my spirited renditions in the car, but they have now grown to appreciate my fine harmonies and say nothing. But I was not hearing the young man's melody and couldn't join his celebration. He looked ridiculous to me only because I couldn't hear his music.

Those of us who are Christian are hearing a different melody than the rest of the world. Our song of grace is unlike any song in the annals of mankind. And the reason our religious gyrations look foolish to the world's citizens is that they are not hearing the rhythm with us. Were they to know of a cross and vacant tomb, of forgiveness and reconciliation, of the eternal party inaugurated by a carpenter, surely they too would tap and sway and nod. All of our strange movements—whispering to Someone unseen, drinking wine and nibbling bread, giving our money to the poor, submitting to baptism, worshiping with friends, and all the rest—would make sense to them if they could only hear the music we're hearing.

But let's be honest—we don't always hear the music either. Sometimes the heavenly tune is so distant we're not even sure ourselves if it is real. God can seem so remote at times that if we dance at all we dance in the silence. The Bible seems dusty, prayer a pipe dream, worship an irrelevant exercise, Christianity itself a fairy tale. The music we have claimed as our source of life and cause for dancing is muffled at times by the deafening absence of God.

It seems inevitable that the parade pass through the desert. Even those who are most spiritual, and know the steps to the dance better than the rest of us, go through dry times and dark nights when there is hardly a hint of music. In fact, those who possess unusual spiritual depth seem to be the best candidates for this arid condition. Those content to skate along the surface of spiritual truth seldom pass through the desert. As Fred Craddock comments, "There are no sea storms in roadside puddles."[1] But those wanting a true relationship with God often experience the absence of the music, the dust of the desert, and spiritual storms that wrack their souls.

This is no new condition. This yearning for God in the silence is at least as old as the Old Testament. Lest we think our periodic dances with no music a modem phenomenon, we need a refresher course in the Psalms. The psalmists over and over pleaded for the music, for God to get with the program and *do something*.

A good case in point is Psalm 42. There is an unmistakable tension in this psalm between belief and unbelief, faith and depression, music and silence. Read it carefully and feel the struggle going on in the psalmist's soul.

1. As the deer pants for streams of water, so my soul pants for you, O God.
2. My soul thirsts for God, for the living God. When can I go and meet with God?
3. My tears have been my food day and night, while men say to me all day long, "Where is your God?"
4. These things I remember as I pour out my soul: how I used to go with the multitude, leading the procession to the house of God, with shouts of joy and thanksgiving among the festive throng.
5. Why are you downcast, O my soul? Why so disturbed within me? Put your hope in God, for I will yet praise him, my Savior and my God.
6. My soul is downcast within me; therefore I will remember you from the land of Jordan, the heights of Hermon—from Mount Mizar.
7. Deep calls to deep in the roar of your waterfalls; all your waves and breakers have swept over me.
8. By day the Lord directs his love, at night his song is with me— a prayer to the God of my life.

9. I say to my God my Rock, "Why have you forgotten me? Why must I go about mourning, oppressed by the enemy?"

10. My bones suffer mortal agony as my foes taunt me, saying to me all day long, "Where is your God?"

11. Why are you downcast, O my soul? Why so disturbed within me? Put your hope in God, for I will yet praise him, my Savior and my God.

Those words are as modern as the latest entry in my spiritual journal. In honestly baring his soul in that psalm, the ancient writer gives us a mirror in which we can better glimpse our own reflection. His feelings are *our* feelings.

He knows, even as we do, that his deepest craving is for God: "My soul pants after you, O God. My soul thirsts for God, for the living God." This unnamed poet knows that he needs more than a new exercise program, more than a new circle of friends, more than exhilarating entertainment, more than psychotherapy. He needs God. Those other things might benefit him some, but they cannot quench his deepest thirst.

There is a God-shaped hole within us that can be filled only by the divine:

> There lives in us, deep down in the heart, a little nightingale that keeps calling for its birdseed. It is a bothersome but infinitely precious little bird. The nightingale lives way down under a host of larger, louder animals, each demanding its food; so it is easy to ignore. It has a "still, small voice." But when we ignore it, even if we feed all the other animals (which is impossible), we are not satisfied, because we *are* that nightingale and we are starving.[2]

Give the psalmist credit for this: At least he knows he's starving, and he knows that only God can satisfy his hunger. Like the Preacher in Ecclesiastes, he is aware that all else is vanity.

It is his craving for God, in truth, that causes his agony. His words reek of depression. Tears have been his companion day and night, he says. The waves and breakers crash over his head, leaving him gasping for breath. He feels forgotten by his Creator. He wonders how a fine, upstanding man of God can sink so low. Twice in the psalm he peers within and wonders, "Why are you downcast, O my soul? Why so disturbed within me?" How can a man of faith, he thinks, be so depressed? On an emotional scale of one to ten, the psalmist rates about a two.

And his reason for gloom? Look again at his words, and you'll find it. He is downcast because God is not doing anything noticeable. In the midst of the darkness, God offers not so much as a flashlight! It is the excruciating silence of God that has battered him into depression.

Cynics come and ask him sarcastically, "Where is your God?"

"I don't know," the psalmist can only say, "but I still trust him."

"Have you seen him lately?" one asks with a wink at his comrades.

"No, I've never seen him exactly, but..."

"Have you ever heard his voice?"

"Well, no, he doesn't really talk aloud..."

"Do you always get what you pray for?"

"No, I suppose not, but he does answer my prayers. I know he does."

"Sure he does," the cynics say as they swagger off. "And the moon is made of green cheese too."

The pitiful man of faith can offer no rebuttal to their doubt. His God is hidden, tucked away in hunches, mystery, and teardrops. How can you verify those things to unbelieving cynics?

So his soul is downcast—but not defeated. The psalm limps at times, but at times it skips. There is yet a glimmer of hope in the poet's heart. He still has a few arrows in his quiver he can use to combat the darkness. Or, to use an analogy more appropriate to the theme of this book, he still has some quarters in his pocket—quarters he can feed into the jukebox to keep the music going.

For one thing, he has memory. Even in the darkness he can remember: "I used to go with the multitude, leading the procession to the house of God, with shouts of joy and thanksgiving among the festive throng." The disconsolate psalmist remembers a procession to the house of God with his friends—the noise, the laughter, the keeping of holy-day. And it is out of a memory like that that hope springs. Hope lives out of memory.

An old song said, "Catch a falling star and put it in your pocket. Save it for a rainy day." Wise people catch memories, like stars, and save them for drizzly nights of the soul. If your pocket is full, you can survive in the darkness.

When, like the psalmist, my soul is cast down, I am grateful for memory. My pocket is crammed with stars:

- Waking, as a teenager, on Saturday morning to the smell of bacon frying and the sound of mother humming, and feeling tears of happiness welling in my eyes.
- My dad greeting me nearly every morning with the sports page and a cup of hot tea.
- Stuttering, quivery-voiced, my proposal to Sherry (I had three sermonic points) under a starry sky in Dayton, Texas, and her immediate acceptance, and my mingled relief and excitement.
- Disillusionment with seminary, with self, with God, but living through that misery to find a new and deeper commitment.
- Sleeping all night in a hospital waiting room, being paged, and stumbling into the hall to see my daughter for the first time—a tiny, chalky-white creature curled in Sherry's arms.
- The calloused hands of old farmers on my head, ordaining me to the ministry of the gospel in a white clapboard church house one hot, Sunday afternoon.
- Books that challenged and thrilled me, not only with their substance but also with their style.
- My embarrassed son receiving the Most Valuable Player trophy from his Pee-Wee League baseball coach and my throat feeling like a hard ball was suddenly lodged in it.
- The long-prayed-over moment of decision when I had to do something, and a door immediately opened, and God seemed so near I could touch him.

The list could go on, but suffice it to say, I know why the ancient writer called upon memory in his hour of need. It is a comforting friend when life gets dreary. That is why the loss of memory by elderly people is such a tragic thing. When they lose their memory, their pockets are empty, and they have no resource with which to summon hope. Without memory, depression is inevitable.

The finest gift we can give our children, I believe now, is memories. If I, as a father, can fashion Stacy and Randel some fond remembrances, I will have equipped them for the darkness. If they will be able to say, "Do you remember the time when Dad...? Do you remember when the dog died and we all cried...? Do you recall the time the four of us worshiped at the lake house...?" If I can give them reasons to remember, I will declare my fatherhood a whopping success.

Imagine you are cut off from civilization, imprisoned in a foreign country. Isolated in a dark, damp cell and bored to tears, you struggle to keep your sanity. Do you know what will keep you alive in that misery? Certainly the scraps of food given you by your captors will help. But those scraps will not be enough. Man cannot live by bread alone. You will be kept alive by memory. If you can remember your dreams, the touch of your lover's hand, the feel of your mattress back home, the laughter of your children—you will survive. If you do not have those memories, your captors can feed you sirloin steak, and you will still perish.

It should not surprise us, then, to find the psalmist reaching for memory in his distress. He will remember that holy festivity of long ago, and he will hear again the faint strains of music.

But the psalmist also calls upon trust—plain, old-fashioned faith—in his hour of darkness. Memory will come to his aid, and so will trust. He trusts God even without *feeling* like it: "By day the LORD directs his love, at night his song is with me—a prayer to the God of my life."

Thankfully, his relationship with God doesn't rest on his moods. His foundation is more solid than the shifting sands of his emotions. He stands on a foundation of commanded lovingkindness and promised evening songs. His faith is in a good God, not his fluctuating feelings.

Even in the night he expects a song. The nighttime heightens every malady. Monsters appear in the darkness that would never surface in the light of day. An hour of nocturnal agony spent pacing, worrying, tossing wide-eyed in bed, or whatever, is worth at least three hours of daytime misery. And foreboding sounds in the night can strike fear into the calmest heart.

But the nighttime sound the psalmist anticipates is the divine melody of assurance. He trusts that when the going gets the roughest, when the night gets the blackest, God will appear with a song to make it all bearable.

And he trusts, too, that the sun will shine again, that the darkness will not be eternal: "...for I will yet praise him, my Savior and my God." There is coming a day, he writes twice in the psalm, when I will break forth in song and praise God for his goodness. Not now, he knows, but the day of dancing is coming.

Whenever we sit in the darkness, the darkness is all we can see. Black obscures all of the other shades in life's prism. We feel alone, confused, terrified, and dejected and believe we will feel this torment all our days. We see ourselves "downcast" and "disturbed" forever.

But Trust says not to lose our perspective. The sun will shine again. The dark shadow will only last for a season. We shall yet praise him who is our source of life and our God. Trust enables us to cling to a ray of hope when Depression whispers a lie in our ears. We rest not on the deception of our fickle moods but on a God who commands his lovingkindness.

The psalmist also has honesty with which to battle his gloom. Memory, trust, and honesty—these are the three coins he will use to try to keep the music going. His prayer in the psalm epitomizes honesty: "Why have you forgotten me? Why must I go about mourning, oppressed by the enemy?" He is able to express his hurts and doubts openly to God. And the very fact that he could write so candidly of his confusion and suffering bears eloquent testimony to the man's honesty.

Our prayers typically epitomize pious trickery: "Our Heavenly Father, thank you for this beautiful day. Bless all of the missionaries serving on foreign fields. Forgive us our many sins, and grant that we may be more like Jesus. In his blessed name we pray, Amen."

That's not a prayer! That's a recitation of religious clichés! There is not enough honesty in that prayer to lift it to the ceiling, much less to the gates of heaven. In glossing our true feelings, we are only playing games with God and making a mockery of the relationship.

Prayer is bundling up our deepest yearnings, hurts, complaints, and love and dropping them at our Maker's feet. Better to scream "Why have you forgotten me?" than to mouth platitudes that trivialize the most important relationship in our lives. At least our scream is an honest cry from the depths of our being.

In 1963, Bishop John A. T. Robinson ruffled a few theological feathers with his book *Honest to God.* Whatever our feelings about the bishop's controversial conclusions, his quest in the book deserves our applause:

> It is for me a reluctant revolution, whose full extent I have hardly begun to comprehend. I am well aware that much of what I shall seek to say will be seriously misunderstood, and will doubtless deserve to be. Yet I feel impelled to the point where I can do no other. I do not pretend to know the answers in advance. It is much more a matter of sensing certain things on the pulses, of groping forward, almost of being pushed from behind. All I can do is try to be honest—honest to God and about God—and to follow the argument wherever it leads.[3]

Like the bishop, we have a duty to be honest to, and about, God. We do not have to traffic in triteness or claim to know more than we actually do. We only have to be truthful in our dialogue with him, for we dare not construct our life-houses on falsehood.

This unnamed poet of old reminds us that honesty is vital to our spiritual condition. Only in living the truth can we hope to be set free. Dishonesty always ferments into disillusionment.

Did the psalmist escape his gloom? Did he ever hear the music again? We do not know. There is no scriptural clue as to the outcome of the tussle.

But I have a hunch, a hope, that he conquered his depression and that he did, as he envisioned, praise his God again. With those three resources on his side, how could he lose?

And if you and I have memory, trust, and honesty jingling in our pockets, how can we be forever deaf to the music? Even on the darkest night, I believe we'll be able to hear traces of the song.

III.
LEARNING TO DANCE

Indeed, grace is the celebration of life, relentlessly hounding all the noncele-brants of the world. It is a floating, cosmic bash shouting its way through the streets of the universe, flinging the sweetness of its cassations to every window, pounding at every door in a hilarity beyond all liking and happening, until the prodigals come out at last and dance and the elder brothers finally take their fingers out of their ears.

Robert Capon in Between Noon and Three

10.
Go Ahead and Die

There is no shortage of advice these days. Books, magazines, newspapers, and radio and television programs all offer us counsel. Preachers, psychiatrists, nutritionists, politicians, and scores of other experts tell us in authoritative tones what we need to make life better. Friends with good intentions also stand ready to bless us with guidance. We are awash in a sea of suggestions.

The suggestions cluster around the theme of reform. What we need, our sources all say, is personal renovation. Some say we need physical reform: a revolutionary diet, a rigorous exercise program, a healing salve for our arthritis, an energy-building potion for our lethargy. Or we need emotional reform: a relaxation technique, an overhauled self-image, a class in assertiveness. Others preach to us spiritual reform: a new method of Bible study, a meditation routine, evangelism training.

But whether the reform is physical, emotional, or spiritual, these sources all underscore the need for change in our lives. If we would be healthy and whole, they suggest, we need to change. And then they proceed to specify the changes we should make.

While I would not for a moment underestimate the validity of much of this advice, I also cannot put too much stock in it. Like the psalmist in Psalm 42, I believe I need more than minor repair, and the New Testament verifies that belief. The Christian message, at its heart, is not a message of reform. Good advice is one thing; the gospel is another. For the gospel doesn't tell us to change; *it tells us to die*. The most radical self-help book on the shelves tastes like pabulum compared with the message of Jesus and his men. The self-help books prescribe a face-lift; the gospel prescribes a funeral.

Jesus advocated finding life by losing it: "For whoever wants to save his life will lose it, but whoever loses his life for me will find it" (Matt 16:25). He said, "I tell you the truth, unless a kernel of wheat falls to the ground and dies, it remains only a single seed. But if it dies, it produces many seeds" (John 12:24). He was talking about his own pending death in that verse, but he went on to give his death a universal application: "The man who loves his life will lose it, while the man who hates his life in this world will keep it for eternal life" (John 12:25). To loosely paraphrase that statement, "He who protects himself and clutches life will come up empty-handed. He who abandons himself and lets go of his pride will reap life in all of its fullness."

The prerequisite for becoming a follower of Jesus, remember, is death: "If any man would come after me, he must deny himself and take up his cross daily and follow me" (Luke 9:23). The followers of Jesus are required to take up a cross, and crosses are for dying on. Paul said to the Corinthians, "I die daily," and so must we if we are ever to serve Jesus and find the abundant life he promised.

The apostle Paul knew and preached the necessity of death. "I have been crucified with Christ," he said to the Galatians. To the Romans he asked, "Don't you know that all of us who were baptized into Christ Jesus were baptized into his death?" Then to the Corinthians again he issued a death notice to all Christians, "For Christ's love compels us, because we are convinced that one died for all, and therefore all died." All dead, because apart from the death of our Self there can be no resurrection. Death is the indispensable prelude to the dance of new life: "We were therefore buried with him through baptism into death in order that, just as Christ was raised from the dead through the glory of the Father, we too may have new life" (Rom 6:4).

What exactly is this death to which we are called? It is the death of our self, our ego, our pride. We are summoned to deny self and to die, which is a redundancy designed to underscore the importance of the command. Denying self and dying are two ways of stressing the same truth. In denying self, we die—to a compulsive need to look good, be successful, and come out on top. In essence, we die to self-glorification.

Now, while this death is freely chosen, it is a reluctant death for most of us. It is actually a death that *never* comes until we see the futility of everything else. Eventually we may smile on the way to the death chamber, but getting to that point takes a lot of "vanity of vanities, all is vanity." Only after all the face-lifts prove a waste of time will we agree to the funeral.

Certainly nothing in our culture prepares us for this death. Culture's gospel has always been to let the self flourish, to indulge the self with the finer things of life. All of our well-intentioned mentors are telling us to live, to look out for our self, to squeeze life to our bosoms and hold it fast. Only the Christian gospel whispers to us the death message that, ironically, finally enables us to relax and live.

I think there are definite stages we pass through with regard to the self. I make no claims to be a scholarly psychotherapist, and far more competent people than I have proposed theories about the self. But common sense observation can reveal to most of us the hierarchy of stages we move through. I see at least six stages in the development of the self:

(1) *The Pre-Conscious Stage*—As newborn infants we are ignorant of the self and have no knowledge of our separateness from the rest of the world.

(2) *The Discovery Stage*—Early in life, we discover our self and know we have a separate identity. Toes, fingers, voice: we are a distinct self with particular features. And we discover there are other "selves" in our world.

(3) *The Protection Stage*—Even as young children, we learn the necessity of protecting our self. We come to see self as a fragile thing that can be easily hurt, so we clutch self and self's appendages. "It's my toy, my turn, my place," we scream as we try to look out for a developing, but flimsy, identity.

(4) *The Disappointment Stage*—Somewhere in late childhood or early adolescence, giant feelings of inadequacy swallow us. Our self is not what it should be, and we are disappointed. Our nose is big. Our skin is dotted with hideous bumps. Our personality is drab. The opposite sex turns away in disgust. We'd like to swap our self for a better model.

(5) *The Acceptance Stage*—At last we get to the point where we can accept our self. We've discovered it, protected it, been disappointed by it, but finally we learn to accept it and present it to the world. We know it is by no means perfect, but we are stuck with a less-than-ideal self and learn to live with it.

(6) *The Magnification Stage*—Having learned to accept our self, we then move to an effort to magnify it. We polish it, coddle it, and want it to be impressive at all times. We have arrived, after a long and painful ordeal, at being able to magnify our self.

It seems to me that culture's gospel stops with stage six. Of course, few are so blatant as to preach self-glorification, but that is the obvious intent of our education and early training. We are all taught to be "successful," and success, by society's definition, is having an attractive self. Whether or not self-magnification is articulated, it is certainly "caught."

But if I understand the New Testament, it is building a seventh rung on the stages of self: *The Death Stage.* We do not have to stop at magnification, I hear it say. There is another step, available to any explorer with the courage to venture higher. It is possible to crucify self and find a joy in life that transcends anything the "looking out for number one" people will ever know. The gospel writers say what to most in our narcissistic society is absolute nonsense: You can't find life until you die.

That message of death sounds horrible to us because it strips us of our power. Our whole society rotates around the struggle for power, and we have been trained since birth to enter the fray. Check the books in the business, psychology, and religion sections of your local library, and you will discover our obsession with power. Books on controlling others, pulling strings, making deals, and selling oneself to the public consistently do well in the marketplace.

And thousands of Americans are graduates of assertiveness training seminars and have mastered the art of getting their "fair share." Because of this training, they will not be shoved around by anyone. They have learned to push and shove too, to shout their rights as loud as the next person. Assertiveness is a power technique, a method for gaining power in relationships.

Even those who pledge allegiance to Jesus have joined the power struggle. Jesus himself refused to be sucked into this "selfish" quest for power:

> During the last hours of his life, Jesus shows a complete disregard for the normal instincts of power-driven personalities. To most of us it matters that people know who and what we are—especially that we are right (the corollary being that others are wrong). We cannot bear to lose; winning is everything. Jesus is so very right, his accusers so very wrong; yet he dies without defending himself.[1]

But we his people have not been so adamant in rejecting power and the feeling of control and success it gives us:

> We are so concerned to show the world what a good life Christians have, and thus to prove to them that they should join up, that we have

decided that the end absolutely justifies the means. And the means is power. Christian organizations spend a lot of money, time, talent, imagination, and energy each year for power. We may call it witnessing, we may call it influence, we may call it using modern technology for Christ's sake. That veneer is certainly present. A scratch will show the veneer for what it is.[2]

Though we have been slow to catch on, what we Christians have actually enrolled in is a lifelong course in submissiveness training: "Your attitude should be the same as that of Christ Jesus: Who, being in very nature God, did not consider equality with God something to be grasped, but made himself nothing, taking the very nature of a servant, being made in human likeness. And being found in appearance as a man, he humbled himself and became obedient to death—even death on a cross!" (Phil 2:5-8).

And I am personally convinced that this submission, this dying to self, this crucifying of pride is crucial to our joy. We think of denying self as somber, grim-faced business when it is in truth a prelude to dancing. If you want power, learn to be assertive. If you want joy, learn to be submissive.

Stop and think for a moment. Isn't it true that our refusal to die has caused most of our misery? We have wreaked untold havoc on ourselves and others by having a big, live self, by insisting we are right, by trying to be in control. We have done no one harm when we died to pride, or admitted our mistake, or loosened up and relaxed. If we could just behave like a good corpse, everybody would be happier for it!

The reason our death increases the joy level all around is that it also increases the love level all around. Only when we die to self can we fully love another. Self is a devilish creature, demanding all of our energy, wanting our constant attention, reaching even into our pocketbooks for favors. How can we be attuned to another's spirit when self is making so much noise? How can we ever hope to love another when self screams for our constant care? When self is alive and well, it offers us an all-or-nothing proposition. We either pacify self, or we crucify it.

But if we choose to let self die, we are amazingly free: free to laugh at our flaws, free to know that the universe doesn't revolve around us, free to fail and get up and try again, free to sit loose to life's difficulties, free to love with *self*-less abandon. Our voluntary death changes our whole perspective on life. We are dead, for God's sake, and most of the pressing concerns of the world are trivial to a corpse.

How do we accomplish this liberating death of self, this execution of ego that leads to life? I think we do it a little bit at a time. We inject a little of the fatal potion into our hearts each day and trust that in time the whole self will feel the effects.

I am no expert at dying to self. My own ego rises daily out of the depths like the Loch Ness Monster, scaring me half silly with its ugly pride. My self is alive and kicking and clamoring for more attention. But I am gradually learning to control it. I am trying, like Paul, to die every day.

The personal, daily deaths of which I speak are so trivial, I hesitate to share them. But my fumbling attempts with the potion may inspire you to do a better job of dying than I will ever do. If nothing else, they will help make clear that self-denial is a daily affair accomplished in ordinary circumstances.

Take the toothpaste tube, for example. The age-old tale about couples arguing over the toothpaste tube is no fable at our house. I am a habitual middle-of-the-tube squeezer, and it bothers my wife. She is a careful, bottom-of-the-tube squeezer and periodically calls my attention to the superiority of her method. Of course she is right, but my self is offended nonetheless.

"What difference does it make?" it shouts. "Who cares about a tooth-paste tube when half the world is starving to death! Besides, I have so many wonderful qualities that overshadow this minor defect. Get off my back! And, by the way, you left the cap off of the shampoo last night."

At the first sign of provocation, my self will put up its fists and make ready for battle. But I am choosing to die to that self. "She is right," I'm learning to say. "She is not wanting to criticize or attack you; she is honestly expressing her mind." So I will agree with her completely and try my best to remember to squeeze the tube from the bottom. I will respond in that situation like any good corpse should. I will let my pride and *self*-ishness go.

When my son strikes out or bobbles a grounder, my self feels a twinge of resentment, as if his humanity casts a bad reflection on it. But I will choose to deny that self, pat my son on the back, and remind us both that it's just a game.

When someone questions me about the size of my church, self begs me to pad the figures. After all, on Easter we did have a full house! My self loves to gloat over its successes and always tries to win approval. But I will deny that self and candidly say we are a small group not known for setting growth records. In saying those hard words, that self will die a little more and the chains clamping my ego-centered spirit will loosen a bit.

When I am asked to try something new, something at which I might fail, I will strongly consider doing it. My self despises failure and gorges on achievement. It pleads with me to try only the safe and comfortable. It would not even let me run for class office in high school it so feared defeat. But I will venture into areas where I might fail just to die to that self. I will choose to risk, because risk is an essential ingredient in the death medicine.

When the world's salesmen invite me to "go along to get along," I will reject their sales pitch. Self wants me to fit in, to project a respectable image, to wear the correct fashions, to be part of the herd. My self so worships acceptance it will become a prostitute for a meager token of the world 's affection. But I will refuse the world's proposal. I will die to that approval-craving self and be different.

These deaths and all of the other ones in process now are, as you can see, small ones. I am a novice in the art of dying to self. Of necessity, I take baby steps, for I am not yet ready to run. But those small deaths are gradually eradicating the pride that stifles my gladness. And one of these days I hope to die so completely that I can "bear much fruit."

I know it will take a long time, perhaps a lifetime. No one dies to self overnight. It happens slowly, through those seemingly inconsequential deaths that happen daily. No one knows I'm dying to self, except possibly my wife who has noticed that the toothpaste tube no longer gets squeezed in the middle. But I'm dying nonetheless, and the reward is my joy.

Let others play the power game; I will try to serve. Let others scramble for position and money; I will be content to love my family, pastor my church, and write the truth as I see it. Let others think that self-magnification is the pinnacle of fulfillment; I will believe the gospel and try to step up to self-denial.

Since the whole world is glibly offering you advice, I might as well give you mine. You want joy? Then go ahead and die.

11.
Finding Fascination

This chapter is about play. As such, it may seem out of place, following as it does a chapter on death. Play seems to be a magnification of self, not a death to self. A discussion of play and its benefits smacks of accommodation to a playful, hedonistic society and seems to be the antithesis to self-denial.

But this chapter is situated right where it needs to be. Before I will be able to play, I will need to die to my self. In fact, anyone who plays must first abandon the self, for play is an activity where the self must be lost, forgotten, or, better yet, dead.

Play is an indictment of my self for it has completely different goals. My self values utilitarianism and feels a pressing need to "accomplish something," whereas play has no real goal or purpose. Self loves hurried efficiency, whereas play never looks at watches or keeps schedules. Self thrives on competition and a carefully defined pecking order, while true play (as opposed to modern-day sports) is oblivious to success, if success is measured only against the achievements of others. So, if I will ever play in life, my utilitarian, efficient, successful self will have to die first.

But should we "serious Christians" even address the subject of play? Shouldn't we be addressing more religious themes such as suffering, praying, witnessing, or walking narrow roads that lead to life eternal? No! Suffering, praying, witnessing, and walking narrow roads have a legitimate place in our faith, but so does play. And we've talked much more about those other things than we have play. Even though several theologians have written on the "theology of play," most of us have never considered Christianity and play as compatible bedfellows. We may have even viewed them as archenemies.

But our capacity to play, to sing and laugh and find fascination, is a vital part of the Christian experience. If we who have tasted amazing grace cannot play, who can? And it is no secret why we call our play "recreation." In the selfless act of frolic and fun, we are "recreated":

Play is more than just nonwork. It is one of the pieces in the puzzle of our existence, a place for our excesses and exuberances. It is where life lives in a very special way. It is the time when we forget our problems for a while and remember who we are. Play is more than just a game. It is where you recognize again the supreme importance of life itself. Like a child, you see life as it is and as it was meant to be. In play you can abandon yourself, you can immerse yourself without restraint, you can pierce life's complexities and confusions. You can be whole again without trying.[1]

To "be whole again" is a strangely theological phrase, because once we peel away the veneer of fun we find a strangely theological rationale for it. Play, it turns out, is one of God's tools for re-creating us. Without it our spirits sag: "Without a playful attitude, work is labor, sex is lust, religion is rules. But with play, work becomes a craft, sex becomes love, religion becomes the freedom to be a child in the kingdom."[2]

Now this is no new, avant-garde idea. Plato in his *Laws* said, "Life must be lived as play, playing certain games, singing and dancing." And during the Renaissance, the recreational value of play was known and appreciated. But during and after the Reformation, play fell into disrepute and life became "serious." The new trinity of values became our comrades: Utilitarianism, Efficiency, and Achievement. Since play didn't fit well with those values, it was discarded as a waste of time. Only lazy, unspiritual sorts would want to play.

For centuries now we have idolized that trinity of values. Even our modern amusements and entertainments don't seem to be truly "play-full." Many of us, especially we dedicated, responsible Christians, find it impossible to let go of our selves and frolic like children.

The result of our serious approach to life is sad:

Play is where life lives. Where the game is the game. At its borders, we slip into heresy. Become serious. Lose our sense of humor. Fail to see the incongruities of everything we hold to be important. Right and wrong become problematical. Money, power, position become ends. The game becomes winning. And we lose the good life and the good things that play provides.[3]

The primary good thing that play provides for us is fascination. Play keeps alive within us our capacity for wonder. When we play, we become fascinated by a particular facet of life. Whether we are collecting stamps, hitting a golf ball, strumming the guitar, or sewing a dress, we are absorbed in something that enchants us. The word "fascinate" comes from the Latin word "fascinatus" and literally means "to bewitch" or "to put under a spell." Our play puts us under a life-renewing spell. It hypnotizes us into joy, for our spirits live on enchantment.

Not long ago, I watched a brief news segment on television about a man enthralled with steam engine trains. This man, now in his sixties, has had a lifelong love affair with the old-time steam engines and even bought one of his own some years ago. Occasionally he cranks it up and chugs through his town, waving at wide-eyed children startled by the sight of an old train engine huffing and puffing down their street. When the man spoke to the interviewer about steam engine trains, his whole being quivered with excitement.

The surprising thing about that TV piece was not its subject matter but how it affected me. I felt emotionally uplifted after watching it. My spirits rose considerably, and I later wondered why. Why would a TV spot about a man in love with steam engines make me feel better?

The answer to that question I realize now has to do with the value of play. That man's enchantment with steam engines was a statement of his individuality and an embracing of one of humanity's peculiar inventions: old trains. I believe he is literally re-*created* when he tools around town waving at astonished children or when he tinkers with his "toy" at home. And in just seeing a TV snapshot of a man at play, I was re-*created* a little bit too. His wonder was contagious.

My own play is running. I once scoffed at runners and labeled them crazy. Running seemed to me a monotonous regimen, totally void of fun. I remember telling a friend that I would never be a runner, that I needed a bat, club, or racket in my hand to enjoy exercise.

Then, through a series of events too long to enumerate, I started running. At first it was what I expected: a sweaty, painful ordeal. But I stuck with it anyway, and at some mysterious, undefinable point, running became play for me. It became a time every day to get away from the crowds and sweep the cobwebs from my mind. A time to breeze through the neighborhood waving at friends and smelling the barbecue sizzling on outdoor pits. A time to pray and rediscover God in the stillness. A time to leap curbs, talk to children, and become a child again myself. I think my daily run is one of the most "Christian" things I do.

The Reformation people and their descendants would, no doubt, disagree. They would brand such play as frivolous, as poor stewardship of time. They would quote me Paul's statement about bodily exercise profiting little and then challenge me to spend that time reading the Bible. But I will not be swayed by their argument. I know the value of play, and I know I can never be whole without it.

There is now raging in Texas a heated debate over public education. A specially appointed committee has recommended a more stringent approach to education: longer school year, longer school day, fewer extracurricular activities, less play, and more academics. The rationale for the proposed changes is greater achievement and efficiency. We're falling behind other countries academically, the committee reported, and need to run a tighter educational ship.

The committee's intent is noble, and some of its suggestions are good. Much in our public education system can be improved. But the mentality behind the changes worries me. It seems to bow before that trinity of idols we have worshiped since the Reformation. "We cannot have our children playing," it seems to say, "when we're falling behind the Japanese in math skills. If we're going to compete with the rest of the world, we need to banish play and get earnest about learning. Play is optional; academics are indispensable."

I would like to see us encourage our children to play. Stress academics? Fine. But also stress play. Teach children to laugh, run, shoot marbles, kick soccer balls, bake cakes, collect coins, catch trout. Perhaps it is not the school's responsibility to teach such things, but somebody needs to. And if school is all "higher learning" and no real fun, I have serious doubts about its effectiveness. Are we trying to teach our children academics or abundant living? If we're stuck on academic achievement, by all means scrap play and add more classes. If we're wanting our children to learn abundant living, though, perhaps we should scrap some classes and add more play!

For it is play, wonder, and "bewitchment" that make life worth living. The educators seem to believe that "heavy" education is the key to the abundant life. And the preachers seem to believe that correct theology is the prime ingredient in joy. But you and I know better. We stay alive with fascination. The man I saw on television can, and probably does, live abundantly without a string of academic degrees or an understanding of deep theology. He cannot make it, though, without steam engines. He cannot have the abundant life without his source of fascination.

Contrary to medical experts, the most dangerous disease in our society is neither cancer nor heart ailment, as dreadful as those diseases are. The most devastating illness around is indifference. In the Middle Ages, this condition was known as "acedia" (sloth), and it was listed by the church as one of the seven deadly sins.

The most obvious symptom of "acedia" is a repeated shrug of the shoulders. When one is afflicted with this condition, nothing matters. Lawns go unkept, bread unbaked, children unloved, and steam engines unnoticed. Life is a meaningless and boring puzzle.

When acedia gets in its advanced stages, a person is powerless to do much of anything. Like a malnourished child too weak to brush the flies from his face, the person with severe acedia is too apathetic to see wonder in even life's finest treasures. Sunsets bring no awe, good music stirs no heartstrings, and freckle-faced little girls evoke no chuckles. The medical examiner would never officially declare it, but the person who gets to that point is dead. There is no telling how many dead people are walking the streets today. "Acedia" is lethal!

The antidote for the disease is the fascination we find in play. As we begin to care about things—tennis, chess, old books, baseball cards, stamps, African violets, or anything else that catches our fancy—we will find the way to smother "acedia." Once we learn to play, we have the ready antidote to depression. We always have a corner of the world we can run to and find delight, even though apathy is taking its toll on those around us.

Play, when you unravel it to its core, is really a statement of caring. When we play we issue a proclamation of loving wonder. Whatever our enchantment, be it old trains or jogging through the neighborhood, we are saying we care:

> The tinfoil collectors and the fancy ribbon savers may be absurd, but they're not crazy. They are the ones who still retain the capacity for wonder that is the root of caring. When a little boy finds an old electric motor on a junk heap, he is pierced to the heart by the weight, the windings, and the silent turning of it. When he gets home, his mother tells him to throw it out. Most likely he will cry. It is his first and truest reaction to the affluent society. He usually forgets it, but we shouldn't. He is sane; society isn't. He possesses because he cares. We don't.[4]

Therefore I offer a chorus of resounding cheers for all who, like the little boy with his motor, really care and know how to play—

The fisherman tying his own flies;
the housewife making apple strudel from scratch;
the nursing home lady hand-painting her china.

The aspiring tennis pro perfecting his topspin;
  the gardener in baggy breeches pruning his roses;
    the kindergarteners skipping rope and singing rhymes on the
    schoolyard.

The infant playing with her toes;
  the photographer painstakingly developing his own pictures;
    and last, but certainly not least, the gentleman
    whistling around town in his steam engine train.

All of them have one thing in common: They're thumbing their noses at "acedia."

12.
Listening to Our Heart

The little boy next door had heart surgery two weeks ago. John was born with a defective valve in his heart, but the doctors decided to wait until he got older and stronger to do the necessary operation. When he turned six a few months back, the heart specialist declared him big enough for the ordeal. Dr. Denton Cooley, the famed heart surgeon, patched the valve in his heart, and now, just fourteen days after surgery, John is running around the neighborhood again, climbing trees.

Before his surgery, a nurse in our church loaned John a stethoscope so he could hear the "before" and "after" sound of his heartbeat. Before surgery, his father told me, his heart made a rattling sound, like a skeleton clattering in a soft wind. After surgery, his heart played the normal sound of a distant tom-tom, steady and slow. John was astonished at the sounds in the stethoscope.

I tell you John's story not because it displays the marvels of modern medicine or because it has such a happy ending. I tell you his story because it holds a clue to our quest for joy. Like John, we must learn to listen to our heart. The secret of joy is there. There is no outside "guru" who can teach us to dance. No psychiatrist. No preacher. No parent. No friend. No writer of books on happiness. The best they can do for us is be honest, report to us where they discovered gladness, and then leave us to our own treasure hunt. For joy is not a "program"; it cannot be conjured with techniques or learned in seminars. Joy can only be discovered in the stethoscope. If we ever hope to find that elusive, abundant life of which Jesus spoke, we will have to listen to our heart.

Certainly when we put our ear to the stethoscope we will hear, like John, that our heartbeat is defective. Sin and self throw the rhythm off and make its throbbing irregular. Ours is not a perfect heart by a long shot. But still, that sick heart of ours is our wisest counselor, our best source of advice, our truest friend:

To what, you ask, can I turn now? Where am I to search? Which guru or authority or spiritual salesman should I listen to?

To your own heart. It is a teacher you can trust, for it will not despise you (it *is* you), and it is wiser than you think. Listen to your heart. It will tell you for what you may hope; it will tell you "the end of humanity" if only you listen deeply. It will tell you of heaven.[1]

I have spent an entire book trying to make the Good News good again, trying to help you dance. I have suggested some theological underpinnings for joy. I have warned you of some of the obstacles to joy I have found. I have even been so bold as to lead you onto the dance floor and try to show you a couple of the steps I have learned. But the truth is, I cannot teach you to dance. And the reason for that is this: I am not hearing your music. I am hearing, faintly, my heart's music, and it is a thrilling melody. But your heart is playing a different tune, and if you desire joy, you will have to hear that tune and step to its rhythm. Joy, you see, is always self-taught.

It took me about thirty-five years to hear my heartbeat, and I am still unaccustomed to its sound. I have not yet learned the melody by memory. But I do know that it plays a strange, haunting tune unlike anything I've ever heard, and when I've heard it best and responded to it most, I've been able to dance with abandon.

What I *have* always had an ear for, though, is the melody of outside musicians. I have read books, heard sermons, attended seminars, and taken to heart all of the advice offered me. Where that advice took me was to the easy, comforting land of conformity.

"Fit in," the lyrics went. "Here's the guaranteed, universal plan for happiness. Cast your lot with the masses, for that many people just can't be wrong." So, I cast my lot with the masses, enrolled in the world-wide school of joy, and never thought once about listening to my heart.

The universal plan for my gladness had in its curriculum football, among other things. Glamour and girls went with the sport, its catalog said. So I played football. My senior year in high school I weighed, after months of weight lifting and gorging on milk shakes, a whopping 145 pounds. As a defensive back, I did not exactly cause panic in the running backs who broke into the secondary. I had fragile bones, a "trick" knee, terrible vision, and a carefully concealed fear of physical contact. But the popular program for my gladness necessitated football and all of its attendant benefits, so I did my best.

The plan also called for gregarious participation in groups. Happiness was found in personal relationships, in "being involved." So I became a "joiner." In both high school and college I felt compelled to join clubs, attend social functions, slap backs, greet strangers, and be an outgoing person. One of my secret fears in college was that I would have no list of activities and achievements underneath my picture in the school yearbook. I worked hard to make sure that didn't happen. Since the universal plan for joy called for friendliness and group activity, I assumed the role of gregarious participant.

Aggression was also on the agenda. "Joy," the textbook said, "is for those who seize it. Only those who have zest and energy will be successful. Seek action. Express yourself. Stand up to people. Don't get pushed around. Claim what is rightfully yours. No one will give you anything." So I tried to be aggressive, to assert myself, to appear confident.

The plan also had a precise curriculum on "spiritual things." It spelled out in minute detail how God bestows the abundant life upon us. Since I have always wanted to be a "serious Christian," I was especially attuned to this part of the universal program for personal delight.

"Pray without ceasing," it said. "Spend hours in prayer, and joy will be your reward. Read the Bible daily and know it by memory. It will take you to ecstasy." I, therefore, prayed until my knees got sore and did my daily Bible readings without fail.

"Going to church," the plan specified, "is a necessity. The Bible says, 'Let us not forsake the assembling of ourselves together.' Sunday school classes, public worship, committee meetings, and building programs will enhance your life and build God's kingdom." Naturally, I took the cue and have been a devoted church person all of my life.

"Evangelism," the plan continued, "is winning people to Jesus. Brush up on your persuasion techniques. Take a course in salesmanship. Confront people with the gospel boldly, and you will reap a spiritual harvest." As I mentioned earlier, I have always wanted to be an effective evangelist and have felt a continuing need to do some "harvesting."

"Preaching," the program said in a special section for the clergy, "is an exercise in asserting authority. Joy comes when you proclaim the Word of God with power. You are God's chosen vessel and must speak with a heavenly unction. You must never confess to doubt or ignorance, for those confessions undermine your authority. And the world is hungry for a man of God who will speak with certainty." Since that was in the plan, I followed it precisely. I prepared biblical sermons. Presented three irrefutable points. Never admitted my humanity. Affected an air of confident piety.

"The gospel," said the common agenda, "is a set of guidelines for living, a sort of checklist for winning the favor of God. It tells what God requires of us, and we must press and strain to meet those divine requirements. The gospel is a God-given taskmaster to keep our sinful spirits from running wild." As I have said throughout this book, "pressing" and "straining" to win the heavenly prize have been my lifelong trademarks.

There were dozens of other prescribed items in the manual of joy— too many, in fact, to mention in one chapter of a book. They were never written anywhere, at least not all of them in one place. But it was easy to piece together the popular plan for finding delight. And I listened closely, tried them all, and found to my disbelief something other than abundant living. What I found after sampling all of the recommended steps to joy was the boredom of conformity.

To put it mildly, it was a disillusioning discovery. When the author of the best-selling book on happiness leaves you empty, where can you turn? When the world-renowned "spiritual giant" cannot lead you to living water, who can? I was Thomas asking the question, "How can we know the way?" I was Peter wanting to know, "Lord, to whom shall we go?"

Finally, I started listening to my heart. After thirty plus years of living by the universal plan, I tried one of my own. Alfred North Whitehead once said that when a man is lost his chief question is not where he is but where the others are. After years of trying to see where others were, I put the stethoscope on and waited for the sound of a heartbeat. And like John, I was astonished at what I heard.

Would you believe my heart said I should give up my dream of playing in the National Football League? That I was never meant to hit people and be mean? That my temperament and body build were not suited for the game? It told me I should have spent my high school years hitting a golf ball or running the mile.

Would you believe my heart said I would never be a "group person"? It told me, as painful as it is to accept it, that I am a loner who cannot thrive in a crowd. It said to foster a few special relationships and guard my solitude.

Would you believe the sound in the stethoscope cautioned me *against* aggression? It called me to a life of submission, said I was built for flight, not fight. It said to quit pushing, to let life happen and others *be*.

Would you ever guess that when I listened closely I heard my heart thump out a spirituality unlike anything printed in the popular manual?

It sang of prayer as brief and frequent conversations with God through the day, not as a long, agonizing ordeal. It said God is my closest companion, close enough to hear and love my whispers of contentment and whimpers of pain. "Pray without ceasing," it sang, but with a different, lilted melody.

It spoke of the Bible as a source book of faith, honestly recording the spiritual adventures and misadventures of ancient people. It said some of the Bible is thrilling to read, but that some of it is boring and some of it completely incomprehensible. It told me to worship the God of the Bible, not the Bible itself.

My heart sang of the church with notes strange to my orthodox ears. "The church," it said, "is not always steeples and institutional structures. You might find church under the steeple, but you might also find church at the old cafe where you and a couple of friends eat barbecue, talk theology and country music, and lift one another's spirits."

It sang to me too of evangelism and said that bearing Christian witness is not pushing Jesus with salesmanship; it is seeing individual people and knowing their names and trying to put a little of Jesus' love in their lives.

When I looked in my heart for wisdom about my calling to preach the Good News, it told me to forget authority and to be real. It suggested that I strip myself of authority and be a servant of the Word. It ordered me to throw away my three-point sermons spiced with clever stories from illustration books and to tell how it is with me, to speak of my own faltering journey on Christ's way.

And when my heart sang to me of the gospel, it sang not of duty and obligation, but of an end to the need for such things. It told me that Jesus had met God's requirements, that he had died to keep me from having to "press" and "strain." It sang to me of a life of dancing, and this book is a result of its music.

Can you believe a heart would say such things? That it would have the audacity to fly in the face of tradition and contradict the universal manual of joy? I was, and still am, shocked myself. I still have to slip on the stethoscope daily to make sure of its sounds. But they are there, and I have heard them enough now to recognize them as my authentic heartbeats.

Following my heart has moved me toward joy. I'm not sure that we will ever know unbridled joy this side of eternity. When anyone promises us a scheme for constant ecstasy, we can be fairly certain that person can't actually deliver the goods. God may keep us a little thirsty here, I think, just so we'll fully appreciate the water from the crystal river on the other side. But I know this much: My heart has been the source of my greatest gladness. And I'm learning to trust it more and more.

So why don't we listen to our heart? Why do we keep turning to outside sources to learn about our own joy? After sifting through all of the possible answers to those questions, I have decided the answer can be reduced to one word: fear. We are afraid of our heart. Afraid of the melody of freedom we hear there. Afraid, too, of the responsibility for our own joy that our heart gives us.

It is safer, you see, to have an external authority. As long as the plan comes from the universal curriculum, or the self-help book, or the preacher, or our parents, we can always blame them when it doesn't work. We can try the prescribed steps; if they don't work, we can discard them and hunt for some other strategy. We can actually spend our whole lives testing and discarding theories, every time mumbling our "vanity of vanities" with the Preacher in Ecclesiastes.

But if we choose to listen to our heart we risk everything. What if we listen and hear nothing? Or what if we hear and don't have the courage to obey? Or what if we do obey and don't find the joy we crave? Or what if we obey and find joy but reap the scorn of others? Sticking the stethoscope in our ears is risky, risky business. We have to listen, obey, accept responsibility, and look freedom right in the eye once we decide to hear and heed our heart.

But it is the only way to learn the tune that can make us dance. Until we know that, we will flit from tune to tune, trying to find the song. We will be spiritual bees dipping into a dozen different flowers for nectar. And we will never be at peace. We will play football when we ought to be running marathons, go to conferences when we need to be walking in the woods, venture the traveled path when we ought to be exploring virgin land. And we will be continually disillusioned with our lives because we're tuning in on someone else's music.

Of all people, we Christians should know and believe the necessity of listening to our heart. We are the people who believe in the Holy Spirit, that gift of God to all believers whom Scripture declares will lead us to truth. We have always given lip service to the presence of the Spirit in our lives but then turn, amazingly, to outside "gurus" to learn about joy. We do not trust the internal authority God has given to point us to the truth. Our trust, it seems, is in the advice of the newspaper columnist or the latest theory from the neighbor next door.

The columnist and the neighbor, for all their good intentions, cannot speak authoritatively about our lives because they live in a different world than we do. Years ago on radio there was a program called "Duffy's Tavern," which featured a bartender-philosopher named Archie. One of Archie's customers was a simple-minded, friendly chap named Finnegan. Often Finnegan would greet Archie with this question: "How are things in the world, Arch?" And Archie would invariably reply, "Your world or ours, Finnegan?"

Archie was right: Finnegan was in his own world. But so are the rest of us. We all see life through unique eyes. We all bear the image of God in a special way. Like snowflakes and fingerprints, no two of us match. Every human heart, in other words, plays a different song.

The secret to joy for each of us is to live gladly in our own world, to hear our own song, to listen in the stillness for that divinely implanted melody that only our heart plays. When we hear that song, it will tell us of joy.

Listen, then. If you will ever dance in life, listen. Shut out the blaring noises of the world's advice-givers and listen.

Listen to your heart. It will give you reason to dance.

13.
The Wind Beneath Our Wings

As I come to the close of this book I feel a growing desire to define joy, to pin the elusive butterfly on a piece of cardboard so we can examine and label it. I sense that I have cast a dozen different flashlight beams in its direction, but that it has fluttered by still unnamed and unexplained. Any book about joy should at least make an attempt to define its subject. And any dance instructor worth listening to knows, at the very minimum, the name of the dance he teaches.

The dictionary is little help. It defines joy as "a very glad feeling; happiness; great delight; pleasure." That somehow gets the lyrics but misses the tune. That same dictionary defines a tear as "a drop of salty fluid secreted by the lachrymal gland," and all of us who have wept in either grief or gladness know that those words don't come close to capturing the true meaning of a tear. If we are ever to catch joy and pin it down, I think we will have to find a better net than a dictionary.

I tried some months ago to capture joy in a sermon. I made a sharp distinction in the sermon between happiness and joy and asserted that happiness is the product of circumstance while joy is the product of surrender. I said that happiness comes when the events of our lives are positive: our health is good, the kids are prospering, the marriage is going well. I maintained that joy comes when we abandon ourselves to God; joy can be ours even when we are surrounded by terrible circumstances.

I thought it was a profound sermon at the time, and I still believe its premise is true. Joy is not synonymous with "smooth sailing," and it *can* be ours even in the worst of situations. In drawing the distinction between joy and happiness I was trying to capture the reality in a sort of negative way by highlighting what joy isn't.

But now that that sermon has simmered awhile, I see that I might have been playing a word game. I think now that it doesn't matter what we call it: joy, happiness, dancing, meaning, a glad feeling, delight, or any number of other possible synonyms. What matters is the reality, not the term used to describe it. It doesn't matter what label we put on the bottle as long as the bottle contains the stuff we need to keep us alive. We can haggle over terms if we wish, but the important thing is to keep the bottle filled! Whatever we call it, we know joy when we taste it, and we know we are dead without it.

When our children were babies we taught them to talk by showing them an object and then putting a word with it. "Lamp," we would say as we pointed to the one by the sofa. "Banana," we would say as we peeled one and handed it to them. "Red," we would announce as we pointed to a ball or mother's lipstick. Our children learned to talk as all children learn to talk, by seeing the reality and then hearing the word society uses to describe it.

That may be the best way to come at joy too. Not to define it, but to point to it and say the word. Trying to capture joy in a definition is like trying to teach a child "red" without a ball or mother's lipstick. It's almost impossible. Can you fathom trying to explain to your baby the meaning of "red" without anything to point to?

So to better illumine this joy I've been writing about, let me try, not to define it, but to point to it, to take you on a casual stroll and show you what the word means. Of necessity the tour will be personal, for as I said in the last chapter, joy is always self-taught and self-discovered. It is probable that some of what I point to as joy in my life will not be joy in yours. But I hope you'll get the idea.

• Do you see that young woman there? The short, hazel-eyed, dark-haired, good-looking one? She's the only woman I ever dated and the only one I've ever loved. She is my wife and my opposite in many ways. Where I am weak, she is strong, and vice versa. But we are partners in the dance of life. We theologize, agonize over the kids, cook hamburgers on the grill, run through the neighborhood, paint the house, mow the grass, and do an assortment of other things together. What she gives me, the feeling I have with her, is joy. There is joy.

• Those children, the ones selling lemonade on the street corner, bear my name too. The blonde is our twelve-year-old daughter, Stacy. Where she got her blonde hair, blue eyes, and cocky personality is a mystery to all of us. Her passion now is track, and her walls are plastered with posters of great runners. She is running the mile on a little track team herself and winning ribbons galore. Where she got that passion and ability is a mystery to no one, though. Her father was quite a speedster in his day too. The chunky, brown-headed boy beside her is our nine-year-old second baseman, Randel. Most valuable player on the Cardinals last year. Lover of baseball and yet, until last summer, sucker of his right thumb. His current passions are the Astros, hot dogs laced with cheese, messy rooms, and irritating his sister. Though they look to all the world like plain, ordinary children, they are a joy. There is joy.

• The old typewriter on the desk over there has seen better days. The local typewriter doctor told me today that its demise is imminent. Its ailments are many: clogged keys, shadowy letters, battered face. But it has served me well. It has faithfully recorded my thoughts and suffered with me through many rejection slips. When the first book saw the light of day, that typewriter and I had some kind of celebration! That old thing, and all it has enabled me to be and do, is a joy. There, as unlikely as it seems, is joy.

• The maroon-and-white running shoes in the closet are new. My knee has been bothering me, so I splurged and bought some good shoes. Six days a week I put them on and jog my miles. If my knee holds up, I'll run my first marathon next winter. This Friday night, the whole family will pile into the car and go to a nearby town for a "Moonlight Madness Run." We'll all run, claim our T-shirts, get some refreshments, and convince each other we're so good we ought to be in the Olympics. Then we'll go home and fall in bed exhausted. But it will be fun. More than that, it will be joy. There is joy.

• The newspaper rolled up on the driveway has long been a friend. Ever since I first learned to read, I have started the day with the sports page. At the age of six, I knew by memory the starting lineup of the Chicago White Sox and checked their box score daily. Thirty years later, I still bounce out of bed each day, motivated by my friend the newspaper. I have a daily regimen that is sacred: arise early before anyone else, make the coffee, fetch the paper, and read and sip in the quiet of the morning. As small as it seems, that regimen is a part of my joy. I could do without my paper and freshly perked coffee, I suppose, but life certainly wouldn't be as enchanting. In a daily routine like that, I find joy. There is joy.

• These books on the shelves beside me are more than books. They are insignias of a pilgrimage, markers of my own journey with God. I love them as I love no other possessions. It would not be stretching the truth to dub myself a "bibliomaniac," a hopelessly hooked "bookaholic." I don't just read books, I notice who wrote them, who published them, how they're put together. In private, I've even been known to smell their pages, for, believe it or not, each book has a unique aroma of paper, ink, and glue. I do not

profess to know much about the arrangements of eternity, but of one thing
I am fairly certain: My heaven will have a bookstore. To crawl into bed with
a finely-polished, stimulating book is one of life's greatest pleasures. It is for
me another example of joy.

• Psychologist Abraham Maslow had a near-fatal heart attack but
recovered completely and was changed in the process. His glimpse at the
face of the Final Enemy freed him to see life through new eyes. He called
it his post-mortem life: "Everything gets doubly precious. You get stabbed
by the very fact of being, of walking and breathing and eating and having
friends. Every single moment of every day is transformed."[1] What he found
in his post-mortem life was joy, joy hiding in the ordinary.

• John Claypool watched helplessly as his ten-year-old daughter, Laura
Lue, battled leukemia. She fought for eighteen months and died. A month
after her death, Claypool stood before his church and preached, of all
things, a sermon of gratitude. In the sermon he said:

> I am here to testify that this (expressing gratitude) is the only way
> down from the Mountain of Loss. I do not mean to say that such a
> perspective makes things easy, for it does not. But at least it makes things
> bearable when I remember that Laura Lue was a gift, pure and simple,
> something I neither earned nor deserved nor had a right to. And when I
> remember that the appropriate response to a gift, even when it is taken
> away, is gratitude, then I am better able to try and thank God that I was
> ever given her in the first place.[2]

When your living room still smells of chrysanthemums and coffee
cake, and your eyes are still wet with tears, and your voice still quivers
when you speak, but you know somehow that you're going to make it and
you can still mumble a word of gratitude, there is only one word to describe
your sorrow: joy. There is joy.

• Even in our jobs, in the "daily grind," we can find it. Wendell Berry
in *The Unsettling of America* writes:

> But is work something we have a right to escape? And can we escape
> it with impunity? We are probably the first entire people ever to think so.
> All the ancient wisdom that has come down to us counsels otherwise. It
> tells us that work is necessary to us, as much a part of our condition as
> mortality; that good work is our salvation and our joy; that shoddy or
> dishonest or self-serving work is our curse and our doom. We have tried

to escape the sweat and sorrow promised in Genesis—only to find that, to do so, we must forswear love and excellence, health and joy.[3]

Joy? Yes! In work that *cares*, that bears the mark of craftsmanship, that is a statement of our style, there is joy.

In the dirt—actual black-sodded ground—you can see it:

> The year after Annie and I were married, the year we first rented this farm, I dug Annie's garden for her; dug it by hand, stepping a spade into the soft black soil, ruining my salesman's hands. After I finished, it rained, an Iowa spring rain as soft as spray from a warm hose. The clods of earth I had dug seemed to melt until the garden leveled out, looking like a patch of black ocean. It was near noon on a gentle Sunday when I walked out to that garden. The soil was soft and my shoes disappeared as I plodded until I was near the center. There I knelt, the soil cool on my knees. I looked up at the low gray sky; the rain had stopped and the only sound was the surrounding trees dripping fragrantly. Suddenly I thrust my hands wrist-deep into the snuffy-black earth. The air was pure. All around me the clean smell of earth and water. Keeping my hands buried I stirred the earth with my fingers and I knew I loved Iowa as much as a man could love a piece of earth.[4]

Joy buried in a plot of Iowa ground? Yes. There is joy.

• Actually it is everywhere, but only a few have eyes to see it. That's why I brought you along. I want you to cultivate an eye for it. And the ones who see it best are the ones who see like children:

> As much in my fifties as in my forties, I feel much of the time like a child. I get excited about the kinds of things that excite a ten-year-old. The first snow of the year, for instance. The smell of breakfast. Buying things, especially books, which, like a child, it is less important for me to read than simply to have. Getting things in the mail. Going to the movies. Having somebody remember my name. Remembering somebody's name. Making a decent forehand in tennis. Being praised. Chocolate ice cream. And so on.[5]

Learn from him. He knows where to look. There is joy.

I suppose the best way to say it is this: Joy is whatever buoys our spirit and helps us soar. The only thread that ties the above examples together is this capacity to lift us off the treadmill of life, this power to make our hearts beat with wonder.

Birds have air sacs all through their body. All they need is a puff of wind in these sacs, and they can fly. I think our spirits have little air sacs all over them too, but without the breeze we never become airborne. Since I will feel a failure if I don't give you some definition of joy, this, then, is it: *Joy is the wind beneath our wings.*

If you accuse me of finding that wind in unusual, even "unspiritual" places, I will readily plead guilty. But I will also caution you to check your theology. If you think that joy should be found only in "spiritual" places— church, ministry, prayer, witnessing—I will have to ask you to check closely for gnosticism. It may have seeped into your theology without you even knowing it.

Gnosticism is an ancient heresy that so accentuates the spiritual that it obliterates the physical. The first-century gnostics firmly believed in ethereal, spiritual realities, but they could not swallow such down-to-earth things as the incarnation: God becoming physical flesh. God, the gnostics believed, would never stoop so low as to reveal himself in physical, material "stuff." Much of the New Testament was written to refute this heresy, but it has persisted in every age.

And it is alive and thriving today, perhaps in us. If we think of God and joy only in terms of "religious things," we are gnostics at heart. If we have a hard time imagining God taking up residence in an old typewriter, or running shoes, or the morning newspaper, or a black dirt farm in Iowa, then, whether we know it or not, we are Christian gnostics. And gnosticism has always been the enemy of gladness. It so "religionizes" joy that it robs it of its meaning. Only when we can see God in all of life, only when we rub out the line between sacred and secular will we truly dance. As William Temple once remarked, "It is a great mistake to think that God is chiefly interested in religion."[6]

What *is* God chiefly interested in? My guess is joy. He wants his people to be free of guilt, free of cumbersome religion, free of empty routine. He wants us to be joyful, to feel the wind beneath our wings.

But we refuse to believe it! We cannot believe the Good News is really that good! We persist in trying to hold on to the old image of God the Loving Tyrant, the Perpetrator of Guilt and Joy-Killing Demands.

C. S. Lewis once wrote some words that all of us "serious Christians" need to hear:

> I know that my tendency to use images like play and dance for the
> highest things is a stumbling-block to you. You... call it "heartless." You

feel it a brutal mockery of every martyr and every slave.... Dance and game *are* frivolous, unimportant down here; for "down here" is not their natural place. Here, they are a moment's rest from the life we were placed here to live. But in this world everything is upside down. That which, if it could be prolonged here, would be a truancy, is likest that which in a better country is the End of ends. Joy is the serious business of heaven.[7]

Since joy is the serious business of heaven, why don't we get a head start? Why don't we go ahead and claim the eternal door prize Jesus promised before he died: "These things have I spoken unto you, that my joy might remain in you, and that your joy might be full" (John 15:11, KJV)? Why don't we quit acting like the Christian Way is a march to the celestial gallows and act, instead, like it's a dance to Zion's eternal fling? Why don't we find those people, those places, those things that put the wind beneath our wings and go there as often as we can?

No less an authority than comic strip theologian Charlie Brown once said, "Joy is the most infallible proof of the presence of God." For once, Charlie is right. Why don't we believe him?

Epilogue:
Dialogue with a Skeptic

Q: I too believe the Christian life should be marked by joy, and God knows I could use more of it myself. But as I read your book, several questions came to my mind that made me uneasy. Can I probe you about a few thoughts?

A: Certainly. That's why I put this epilogue in the book.

Q: Well, there's still something in all of this talk about joy that smells to me of cheap grace. I can't quite escape the idea that the gospel is primarily about radical commitment, not a waltz down Happiness Lane. Isn't this preoccupation with joy just a religious version of hedonism? Aren't we catering to the "looking out for number one" crowd when we try to make the way of the Cross a pleasurable dance?

A: I have two responses to your concern. And by the way, I think your concern is definitely warranted.

First, as I mentioned briefly in the early part of the book, nobody goes far without the motivation only joy can give. If we want to be and do anything worthwhile, we'd better get a good dose of joy in us. For us to say that we should entertain no thoughts of joy is like saying an automobile driver is selfish to think of filling his gas tank. Joy is the essential ingredient in a truly spiritual life. It motivates us to do all of those disciplines that are so important. So I don't think it is hedonistic to want to dance; I think it is imperative.

My second response to your concern is in the form of a rebuttal question: Why, when we talk about "the radical gospel," do we refer only to radical commitment? Why not speak also of radical grace? Certainly the Christian gospel pulls and stretches us into a new shape. It calls for commitment and radical nonconformity. But so often that side of the street, the sideline with duty and commandments, is the only side we work. I worked it pretty hard in a couple of earlier books myself. But why not work the other side of the street too—the side lined with grace, freedom, and the eternal party? If we omit it, we distort the Christian message and make it a heavy, obligatory deal. And that's what I think is happening now in evangelical Christianity. We have worked the radical commitment side so hard we have omitted the radical grace side. And without the grace side, the road is not much fun to travel. Without the grace side, Christianity is that sad march that is so evident now in most churches. The average churchgoer today is a gloomy, weary pilgrim.

Q: But don't you think that some people will read this book and think that the Christian life is just a scheme for happy living and that God exists to make them comfortable and "joyful"?

A: Perhaps. But any writer runs the risk of being misinterpreted. And if anyone takes this book and makes it say that the "good Christian" is always blissfully tiptoeing through the tulips, that person has definitely missed my point. But the risk of being misinterpreted is, in this case, worth taking. For every person who twists my thinking into an egocentric scheme, I hope there will be a dozen faithful marchers who will be set free to dance a little.

Q: I would call myself one of those faithful marchers, I suppose. And I would really like to dance. I know I'm too tight, programmed, and institutionalized. But do you know what I think really keeps me from dancing? I hate to say it because it makes me sound like an atheist or something, but it's the Bible. When I read a book like this I get all excited because the Good News really sounds good! Then I start reading the Bible, which I believe is the inspired Word of God, and it sounds like Bad News with a capital "B." Do you know what I mean?

A: I think so, but elaborate a bit.

Q: So much of the Bible seems to make God a villain. All of those Old Testament passages where he commands the Israelites to slaughter their enemies, for instance. And all of those divinely instituted laws that are so irrelevant and even cruel. I don't know what to do with those passages.

Last year I made a vow to read the Bible from cover to cover. I started in Genesis and planned to read all the way through Revelation. But by the time I finished Leviticus, I was thoroughly depressed. I kept on reading, though, and made it to the twenty-first chapter of Deuteronomy. There God says that a disobedient son is to be taken by his parents to the elders of the city, who are to stone him to death. That did it for me. My read-the-Bible-through-in-a-year project crashed and burned right there. Maybe it's because I have a hard-headed teenage son myself and the passage hit close to home, but I just got disgusted and quit.

Do you see what I mean? Where is the Good News in any of that? How can a God who decrees the stoning of wayward sons be good and loving? I want to believe what you say in this book, but so much of God's Word seems to nullify it.

A: There is no denying that some of the Bible paints a sinister picture of God. But the key to making sense of Scripture is to detect its movements. There is a divine pendulum swinging through the history of mankind and, thus, through the pages of Scripture. If we can see the movement of that pendulum, the Bible will come alive for us.

Take, for example, the law you just mentioned. In Deuteronomy 21, a rebellious son is stoned to death. But in Luke 15, a rebellious son is forgiven and given a lavish party! Obviously, the pendulum moved a long way between Deuteronomy and the Gospels.

And this kind of movement can be detected in a number of areas. There is a movement through Scripture from bondage to liberation; from God as tribal deity to God as universal Father; from keeping the law to receiving grace; from doing battle with enemies to loving them; from polygamy to monogamy; from a select priestly tribe to the priesthood of all believers; from a God who demands sacrifice to a God who makes the ultimate sacrifice himself. The movements are too many to list, but you can get the picture.

The best interpreters of Scripture are the ones who detect these changes, the ones who can see the sweep of Scripture.

Q: That helps me some with Deuteronomy, but there are some awfully sinister passages in the New Testament too.

A: I know, but the pendulum didn't stop swinging in the first century. We Christians typically are guilty of believing in "frozen revelation." We believe that God suddenly got lockjaw after he inspired John to write the last book of the Bible.

But the fallacy in that thinking is readily apparent. Would the God who started the pendulum swinging at the beginning of the human drama decide to stop it centuries before the drama is over? Would God suddenly grow silent and inactive after years of participation with his creation? Of course not. God continued to be active in the world after the biblical canon was closed, and he continues to nudge the pendulum today. He speaks a contemporary word just as surely as he uttered an ancient one.

Q: That seems to destroy biblical authority though. It sounds as if you're implying that my thoughts could be as inspired of God as the thoughts of the New Testament writers. Aren't you suggesting that the Bible is really not the final word?

A: The same Spirit who inspired the biblical writers to put pen to papyrus is still inspiring men and women today. If that is not true, we are fools to write books, preach sermons, tell stories, and whisper prayers. All of those things rest on the belief that God did not quit inspiring man when the canon was closed.

But the Bible will always be authoritative for the Christian community because it records those historical events that make Christianity what it is. If we want to know what God has been up to all these years, if we want to see how the pendulum has moved, there is no better place to go than the Bible.

To be a Christian in today's world means that we become part of the movement, that we go in the direction of the biblical breeze. It does not mean we go back to where the pendulum was in the first century, when women were advised not to speak in church, when man believed in a three-story universe, when slavery was an accepted institution, and so on. To try to go in that direction is to be guilty of freezing the Word of God and not letting it live.

Q: That still sounds like a shaky view of biblical authority to me.

A: I prefer to see it as a healthy respect for the work of God's Spirit. If the Christian life is nothing more than memorizing mandates two thousand years old, it holds little intrigue. But if the Christian life is sensing movement, being alert to what God has been doing since creation, and trying to listen for him now in my own heart, then it is chock-full of adventure. Too many modern Christians look back instead of ahead.

Q: Okay, I'll meditate on that. Let me shift gears and ask you about something else I felt as I read. I thought I noticed a touch of Quietism in you. Some of what you said, especially the part about witnessing, seemed to indicate that we can just sit on our hands and let God strut his stuff. It sounded to me like running from responsibility. Remember, God has committed unto us the ministry of reconciliation. We are the only hands and feet he has in the world.

A: Of course we have responsibility. We have responsibility for building a faith that is real and passionate. We have responsibility for building personal relationships that are full of love and depth. In short, we have a responsibility to live by the great commandment, to love God and people.

But if there is any one thing that can douse our joy it is the conviction that we are indispensable to God, that the whole plan for the human race rests on our devotion. I see Christians all the time who are drained because the burden is too heavy. The salvation of everyone at the office rests on their witness. The ministry of the entire church depends on their faithfulness. Their whole relationship to God is built on the foundation of personal responsibility. And frankly there is no way to dance with the weight of the world on your shoulders.

God is God. He's got the whole world in his hands. If we forget that and start assuming his burdens, we are guaranteed a life of misery. That is why I called admitting our humanity "the crucial confession."

Q: I appreciate your emphasis on the sovereignty of God, but what about those other aspects of God's nature, like his wrath, his judgment, his banishing of unbelievers to hell? You seem to have skirted those characteristics completely.

A: I think those supposedly sinister parts of God's nature are actually indispensable to the Good News.

Q: Would you like to elaborate on that?

A: All right. Let's consider hell. There is no doubt that hell is a biblical idea. Try as we might to erase it from the canon to ease our minds, hell refuses to go away. It is there. Fire. Second death. Outer darkness. Weeping and gnashing of teeth.

But I have come to see hell as part of the Good News because it is an eternal symbol of our freedom. Hell is God's reminder to us that we are free—free to choose life or death, free to choose love or hate, free to choose for him or against him. Hell is absolutely essential in a free universe. If people don't want God they are free to go to hell. And God's judgment and wrath are but the regrettable consequences of our refusal of his love.

We can't, however, blame this situation on God. He has done everything short of coercion to reconcile all mankind to himself. The notion that God sends people to hell is a false one. I think C. S. Lewis got it right when he suggested that in the final accounting there will be two kinds of people: those who say to God, "Thy will be done," and those to whom God sadly says, "*Thy* will be done."

Hell, you see, is not a punitive place created by an angry God. It is a necessary place created by a loving God who stubbornly refuses to override our freedom.

Q: That does get God off the hook, doesn't it?

A: Yes, off the hook and on the cross, so anyone who wants to can come to the party.

Q: What about all of those dedicated Christians who are such miserable people, those who seem so far removed from the party? Would you say they really know God? And, conversely, how about those pagans who seem to be truly joyful? Are the happy pagans closer to the kingdom than the straight-laced saints?

A: Three thoughts come to mind here.

First, don't be fooled by the pagan's happiness. Some who laugh the loudest and seem to really enjoy living are actually empty, desperate people. Peel away the mask and you will not see joy, but terror. Terror because their lives have no spiritual foundation. Terror because their lives have no intimate relationships. Terror because all of their merriment has been in vain. A life apart from God, regardless of appearances to the contrary, is no picnic.

Second, we had better be careful about deciding who is "in" and who is "out." That is God's business, and Jesus said the judgment will be full of surprises. No doubt some of the respectable ones who never miss church are, in reality, far, far from the party. And some who look to us to be rascals of the wildest sort actually are "tuned in" to grace. So, I'm a little leery of anyone who tries to separate the sheep from the goats.

Which leads me to my third thought: Orthodoxy never saved anyone. We think it does, but it doesn't. If our relationship to God depends on our theological correctness, we are all sunk. None of us has it all right. Each church, each denomination dogmatically argues its case and staunchly maintains its infallibility. But the truth is, we're all wrong in one way or another. We are saved by grace. Period. The grocer has showed up and said the groceries are free to any and all takers. We can argue over the best way to shop and how to take care of the bill if we wish, but that doesn't negate the reality of the offer of free groceries. We are saved by grace through faith. Our part is just to have the faith that God will be true to his Word and give us the promised goods. Our questions about heaven and hell, then, usually skirt the main issue. Whether a person is a Sunday school attender or a scoundrel is not the key question. The real question is: Who will accept these groceries with no strings attached?

Q: But don't you think the decision to accept the groceries obligates a person to a life of service and commitment? Doesn't the Christian prove his faith by his works? In other words, the scoundrel can't remain a scoundrel, can he?

A: He will always be a scoundrel, just as you and I will always be scoundrels. We may be respectable, churchgoing scoundrels, but we are scoundrels nonetheless.

But the thrust of your questions is true. God's love changes us. I can't fathom anyone not being shaken to the core if that one really understands the Good News. We have been died for! Christ laid down his life so we could be free. If we understand the Cross and what it means to us, we will be irrevocably changed by it.

The Cross is the one essential ingredient in Christian theology. We Christians chose our symbol well. If we know of the Cross and its implications, I think our theology is impeccable.

Q: That's a pretty simplistic theology, isn't it? What about all of the other doctrines that fill theology books? Aren't they important?

A: I agree with Englishman Colin Morris who once wrote, "Doctrines, however venerable, which cannot be put into action in the work-a-day world can safely be left in the care of the technical theologians who will preserve them in an atmosphere as cold as a refrigerator."[1]

Many of our venerable doctrines have little bearing on the work-a-day world. Most of what we Christians argue about—precisely how God created the world, who wrote certain books of the Bible, the method God used for inspiring the biblical writers, how God will draw the curtain on human history, the best mode of baptism, whether the Book of Jonah is literal or figurative—makes very little difference in the way we live our lives. In other words, you can't take those doctrinal statements and translate them into concrete action.

That's why I say that the Cross is the one essential ingredient in theology. It is readily translatable. The Cross shows us most clearly the love of God, which we can convert into personal joy. And it gives us the ultimate model of self-giving, which we can convert into servanthood. The Cross is the main attraction of Scripture. All the other doctrines are sideshows.

Q: It seems odd to link something as gruesome as a crucifixion with the notion of joy. Are Jesus' death and our dancing really connected?

A: They are inseparable. Jesus died to end all necessity of our doing religion. No piety, sacrifice, theology, or morality is now needed to buy God's favor. The price has been paid for us. We don't have to try to impress God anymore or wonder what he thinks about us. That was settled at the Cross. The Word of the Cross says that nothing we do will impress God so we can quit trying. It says that God is pleased as punch with us so we can start living like it. Really, it's the best news imaginable.

Q: That truly is Good News!

A: Indeed! It's enough to make you want to dance, isn't it?

Q: Yes, it is. But I've been marching so long it may take me awhile to learn the steps.

A: I'm new at it myself and learning slower than I care to admit. But I'm beginning to believe "the abundant life" is more than just a pious phrase intoned by joyless preachers. I'm beginning to think "the abundant life" is a distinct possibility.

Q: I hope you're right. Anyway, thanks for reminding me that joy is supposed to be the trademark of the follower of Jesus. I needed that.

A: I hope the book was stimulating and helpful. I wish for you a future filled with dancing. And if our paths never cross again this side of eternity, I trust we will some day meet and make merry on the streets of Zion.

Notes

Chapter One

1. Quoted in John Killinger, *Bread for the Wilderness, Wine for the Journey* (Waco: Word Books, 1976), 69.
2. Edna Hong, *The Downward Ascent* (Minneapolis: Augsburg Publishing House, 1979), 17.

Chapter Two

1. E. B. White, "International Herald Tribune," July 13, 1968, 16.
2. Henri J. M. Nouwen, *Creative Ministry* (Garden City, New York: Doubleday, 1971), 25.
3. Robert Farrar Capon, *Between Noon and Three* (San Francisco: Harper & Row, 1982), 162–63.

Chapter Three

1. D. Bruce Lockerbie, *The Timeless Moment* (Westchester, Ill.: Cornerstone Books, 1980), 112.
2. Quoted in George Sheehan, *Running and Being* (New York: Warner Books, 1978), 66.
3. Karl A. Olsson, *Come to the Party* (Waco: Word Books, 1972), 76–77.
4. Sheehan, *Running and Being,* 235.
5. Hong, *The Downward Ascent,* 28.

Chapter Four

1. Capon, *Between Noon and Three,* 176–77.

Chapter Five

1. William E. Hull, *Love in Four Dimensions* (Nashville: Broadman Press, 1982), 70.

Chapter Seven

1. Olsson, *Come to the Party,* 48.

Chapter Eight

1. Virginia Stem Owens, *The Total Image* (Grand Rapids: William B. Eerdmans, 1980), 11.
2. Sören Kierkegaard, *Concluding Unscientific Postscript*, translated by David Swenson and Walter Lowrie (Princeton: Princeton University Press, 1941), 55.
3. Fred B. Craddock, *Overhearing the Gospel* (Nashville: Abingdon Press, 1978), 117.
4. Quoted in Owens, *The Total Image*, 53.
5. Henri J. M. Nouwen, *The Way of the Heart* (New York: Ballantine Books, 1981), 39.
6. John Baillie, *Invitation to Pilgrimage* (Grand Rapids: Baker Book House, 1942), 22.

Chapter Nine

1. Craddock, *Overhearing the Gospel*, 98.
2. J. Kreeft, *Heaven: The Heart's Deepest Longing* (San Francisco: Harper & Row, 1980), 116.
3. John A. T. Robinson, *Honest to God* (Philadelphia: Westminster Press, 1963), 27-28.

Chapter Ten

1. Cheryl Forbes, *The Religion of Power* (Grand Rapids: Zondervan, 1983), 117.
2. Ibid., 68.

Chapter Eleven

1. Tim Hansel, *When I Relax I Feel Guilty* (Elgin, Ill.: David C. Cook, 1979), 63.
2. George Sheehan, *This Running Life* (New York: Simon & Schuster, 1980), 134.
3. Sheehan, *Running and Being*, 72.
4. Robert Farrar Capon, *Bed and Board* (New York: Simon & Schuster, 1965), 116.

Chapter Twelve

1. Kreeft, *Heaven*, 17.

Chapter Thirteen

1. Sheehan, *Running and Being*, 197.
2. John Claypool, *Tracks of a Fellow Struggler* (Waco: Word Books, 1974), 82.
3. Wendell Berry, *The Unsettling of America* (New York: Avon Books, 1977), 12.
4. W. P. Kinsella, *Shoeless Joe* (New York: Ballantine Books, 1982), 14.
5. Frederick Buechner, *A Room Called Remember* (San Francisco: Harper & Row, 1984), 183.
6. Quoted in Madeleine L'Engle, *Walking on Water* (New York: Bantam Books, 1980), 132.
7. C. S. Lewis, *Letters to Malcolm: Chiefly on Prayer* (New York: Harcourt, Brace, & World, 1963), 92–93.

Epilogue

1. Colin Morris, *Include Me Out* (Nashville: Abingdon Press, 1968), 36.

www.ingramcontent.com/pod-product-compliance
Lightning Source LLC
LaVergne TN
LVHW051745080426
835511LV00018B/3235